Paul's SAT
기출해설서

Paul Academy

국내최초
한글판 SAT®
해설서!

Part 1_ Test 1
Part 2_ Test 2
Part 3_ Test 3
Part 4_ Test 4

SAT® is a registered trademark of the College Board, which is not affiliated with and does not endorse this product.

Contributors

Written and edited by the talented test prep professionals at
✓ Paul Academy

PaulAcademy is the publishing arm of one of the industry-leading test prep organizations in Asia. PaulAcademy is a dedicated test prep organization that has helped thousands of students to realize their potentials and achieve their dreams. As a leader in test prep & strategy development specializing in SAT, ACT and AP preparation, PaulAcademy teaches pragmatic problem-solving skills that will ultimately help students obtain successful academic results. PaulAcademy aims to spread the expert knowledge to students worldwide.

Editor-in-Chief
Paul Kim

Head of Publishing
No Yong Park

Material Development & Editing
Do Gyun Kim, Young Yoon Kim, HaEun Hailey Sung, Esther Ra, Hye In Choi

Marketing
Byeong Kook Kim, Jae Woo Jung, Joo Yong Lee

Formatting & Design
MONOPY

Email: books@paulacademy.net   Website: http://www.paulacademy.net

Copyright © 2015 All rights reserved by PaulAcademy.
The contents of the book may not be copied or reused without the expressed written consent of PaulAcademy.

"SAT" and "The Official SAT Study Guide" is a trademark of CollegeBoard, which is not affiliated with PaulAcademy.
CollegeBoard does not endorse this product.

ISBN: 979-11-86461-02-0

Paul's SAT 기출 해설서

Paul Academy

Paul's SAT 기출해설서 서문

10여 년 전 "한국의 Test Prep이 세계 최고"라는 가능성을 보고 유학길에 올라 공부를 마치고 귀국 후 강남의 모 SAT 학원 팀장으로 매년 20%씩 성장을 이룬 후, 그 학원을 나와서 '친절한 폴샘'의 SAT 서문을 쓴 지도 이제 2년이 지났다. 그 당시에는 "아마존 Test Prep 분야 넘버원"이라는 꿈을 위해서 한국의 SAT 교재 1등을 달성한 후에 미국에 진출하고 싶다"고 이야기했는데, 그 2년 간 수많은 동역자들의 도움으로 한국 SAT 교재 베스트셀러(교보문고 기준)를 달성했고, 미국 Amazon.com에 진출하여 SAT Grammar 분야 4위, SAT Math 분야 15위를 기록했다. (2015년 5월 25일 기준) 글로벌 시장 진출을 위해서 시리즈 제목도 '친절한 폴샘의 SAT' 시리즈에서 'Paul's SAT', 'Paul's ACT' 시리즈로 정비하고 본격적인 미국 진출에 박차를 가하고 있다.

저자의 고교 시절에는 교과서, 학교 수업과 참고서만으로도 충분히 자기주도학습이 가능했지만, 지금은 학원에서 공부하지 않으면 효율적인 학습과 시험준비가 불가능하다는 견해가 이 사회에 팽배해 있는 것 같다. 저자는 좋은 교재와 콘텐츠를 만들어 사교육에 의존하지 않고도 자기주도학습이 가능하다는 것을 증명하고, 학습에 대한 잘못된 사회인식을 바로잡고, 더 나아가 미국 아마존의 Test Prep 분야에서 세계최고가 되어 '교육한류'의 한 축이 되고 싶다.
만일 누군가 독학이 힘들어 학원의 도움이 필요하다면, 폴아카데미에서 도움을 받기를 바란다. 폴아카데미에서는 본 교재를 사용하여 학생들이 빠른 시간 내에 고득점을 받을 수 있도록 도와주고, 혼자서 해결하기 힘든 부분들에 대한 해결책을 제시해 주고 있다.

이 책은 2015년 6월 30일 출간된 College Board의 SAT Official Guide에 대한 한글판 해설서다. 이전 블루북과는 달리 4개의 Practice Test가 실려있고, 그것에 대한 영문해설이 탑재되어 있다. 본 책에서는 폴아카데미만의 Quick and Easy 솔루션을 제공하고, 모든 문제를 categorize하여 문제를 더 빨리 이해하고 풀이할 수 있도록 도와준다.

본 교재와 콘텐츠를 통해 단기간에 고득점을 가능하게 하고, 그렇게 확보된 소중한 시간을 본인이 진정으로 하고 싶은 것을 하면서 사는 세상을 만드는데 기여하는데 이 책이 좋은 첫걸음이 되길 바란다. "Paul's SAT 기출해설서"가 빛을 볼 수 있도록 많은 사람들이 도움을 주었다. 내게 "best place to work"의 꿈을 심어주신 하늘에 계신 사랑하는 아버지, 못난 아들을 위해 항상 기도해 주시는 사랑하는 어머니, 부족한 남편임에도 열심히 섬겨주는 사랑하는 아내, 그리고 바쁘다는 이유로 함께 시간을 갖지 못해도 바르게 자라주고 있는 사랑하는 두 아들 영준, 경준에게 너무나 고맙고 사랑한다는 말을 전하고 싶다. 마지막으로 길가의 돌멩이보다 못한 나에게 비전을 주시고 여건을 허락해 주신 하나님께 감사를 드린다.

Paul Kim

NYU에서 영어교육을 전공하였으며 실력 있는 SAT, ACT 부문 최고의 전문강사로서 세한아카데미에서 수많은 학생을 가르치며 큰 명성을 쌓아온 Paul Kim은 현재 Test Prep 전문기관 Paul Academy의 대표로 재직하고 있다. Paul Academy에서는 SAT 및 ACT 교재 시리즈 출간, 온라인 교육 콘텐츠 개발, 자기주도학습과 수험생을 위한 영어교육 전반에 힘을 쏟고 있다.

Paul's SAT 기출해설서 교재구성

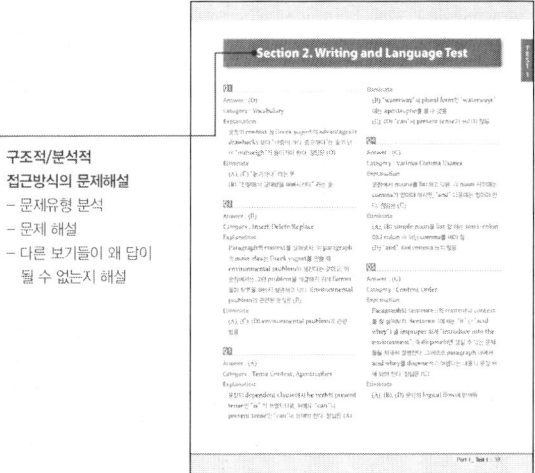

구조적/분석적 접근방식의 문제해설
- 문제유형 분석
- 문제 해설
- 다른 보기들이 왜 답이 될 수 없는지 해설

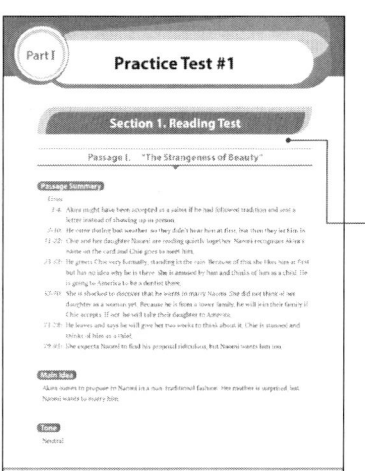

기출지문에 대한 자습서식 풀이
- Passage 요약
- Main Idea
- 어조(Tone)
- 단어/어구 풀이

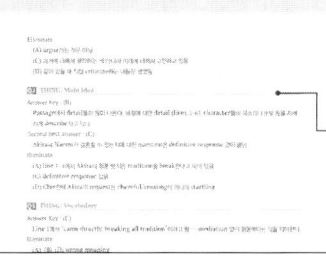

구조적/분석적 접근방식의 문제해설
- THING: 문제출제이유 제시
- 문제유형 분석
- 문제 해설
- 다른 보기들이 왜 답이 될 수 없는지 해설

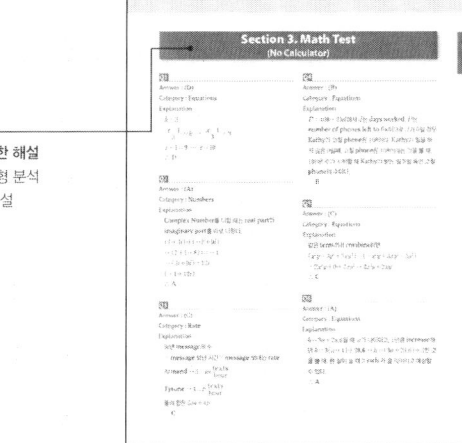

간단명료한 해설
- 문제유형 분석
- 문제 해설

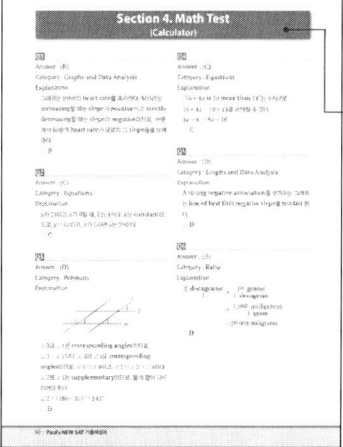

신속하고 정확한 정답 솔루션
- 문제유형 분석
- 문제 해설
- 가장 신속하고 명쾌하게 정답에 도달할 수 있는 solution 제시

SAT 시험, 이렇게 바뀐다!

2016 Redesigned SAT 소개

시행일시 : 2016년 3월부터 시행될 예정

1. Redesigned SAT 주요변화

A. 점수
- 전체 2,400점 만점 → 1,600점 만점 (Reading + Writing & Language 800점, Math 800점)
- 에세이는 선택사항으로 변경되고 점수도 독자적으로 매겨진다. Reading, analysis, writing 각 항목에 대해서 2~8점 배점되고 총점은 24점
- 에세이가 선택사항으로 바뀌었지만 상위권 대학을 희망하는 학생들은 필수적으로 점수를 받아놓아야 한다.

B. 영역
Essay, Critical Reading, Writing, Math 였던 영역구분이
→ Evidence-based Reading & Writing(Reading + Writing & Language), Math, Essay(선택사항) 으로 변경됨

C. 시험시간
전체 3시간 45분이었던 것이 3시간으로 축소. (에세이를 선택할 경우에는 3시간 50분)

1. Evidence-based Reading & Writing:Reading 65분, Writing 35분

2. Math: 55분 계산기 허용, 25분 계산기 사용불가

D. 시험 문제수
- Critical Reading: 67문제 → 52문제
- Writing: 49문제 → 44문제
- Essay: 1문제 그대로
- Math: 54문제 → 58문제

E. 시험 출제방식
- 오지선다에서 사지선다 방식으로 변경
- 지필시험방식을 유지

F. 채점방식 및 기준
- Essay: 글의 일관성보다는 학생의 분석능력과 논증과정을 중시
- 오답에 대한 감점제도 폐지: 틀린 문제와 풀지 않은 문제가 성적에 영향을 주지 않음

G. 기존 SAT와 새로운 SAT 비교표

현재 SAT			2016 Redesigned SAT			
과목	시험시간	문제 수	과목	시험시간	문제 수	시험방식
Critical Reading	70분	67문제	Reading	65분	52문제	4 LP 1 DP
Writing	60분	49문제	Writing & Language	35분	44문제	4 Passages
Essay	25분	1문제	Essay	50분	1문제	1 EP 1 RP
Math	70분	54문제	Math	80분	58문제	계산기/ 38문제 NO계산기/ 20문제
계	225분	171문제	계	180분 (에세이 포함시 230분)	154문제 (에세이 포함시 155문제)	

※참고 – LP: Long Passages, DP: Double Passages, EP: Essay Prompt, RP: Reading Passage

2. 과목별 구체적인 변화

A. Reading Test (독해)

1. 단어의 난이도 보다는 context에 집중
   - 기존의 단어 뜻 모르면 풀 수 없는 obscure한 문제 폐지
   - Extended context에서 단어 톤 찾기
     예) how word choice shapes tone/impact
   - Sentence Completion 폐지
   - 단편적인 정보, 직접적으로 단어 뜻을 물어보는 문제는 축소

2. Analysis & evidence use (분석, 근거 사용)
   - 답을 찾아내는 것뿐 아니라 텍스트의 어느 부분이 그 답을 support하는지 찾아야 한다
     예) Which portion of the passage best supports the answer to the text?
     CB: "There will be at least one question asking them to select a quote from the text that best supports the answer they have chosen in response to the preceding question."

3. Real-world에 관한 지문
   - 기존의 임의적인 토픽의 essay와 fiction은 나오지 않음
   - 차트, 그래프, 인포그래픽이 포함된 지문 (reading, writing, math 모두 동일하게 적용됨)
   - 1개의 역사/사회 지문과 1개의 과학지문

4. 새로운 지문
   - 미국, 세계문학 유지, 역사/사회/과학 지문 추가
   - Founding Documents (미국 건국자들에 관한 문서), Global conversation 지문 포함

학습전략

2016 Revised SAT는 Evidence-based reading을 강조하므로 글의 paragraph summary, main idea, tone을 꼼꼼히 체크해가면서 글을 읽고 이해를 하며, 리딩문제를 풀 때 더 이상 '감'에 의존해서 푸는 것이 아니라 몇 번째 line을 통해서 답을 유추했는지를 항상 확인하면서 공부를 해야 한다. 혼자 하기 어려운 학생은 친절한 폴샘의 기출해설서의 CR 영역을 공부하면 된다.

Passage Reading Q6-24

Short passage 1 Q6-7

Passage Summary
Ln. 1-14 author looks up at the stars and a comet, while horses don't look up at all, which makes him/her feel good to be human (since only humans look up and philosophize about these things)

Tone : happy, appreciative "wonderous" (line 10) "good" (line 12)

Vocabulary and Phrases
Ln. 1 Whistling and moaning 휏바람 불듯 그리고 불평하듯 (바람이) whipped: (채찍을 하듯) 불었다.
Ln. 3 slid a river of clouds that … all day(line4) 엄청난 구름들이 오르락 내리락 하는 모습 설명.
Ln. 5 Comet hale-Bopp hung like … the punishing wind (line7) 혜성 Hale-Bopp이 깃털로 만든 남자의 미끼처럼 하늘에 머있었다. 그 혜성의 꼬리 부분은 바람에 벌을 받아 밀려 약간 휘어있었다. 석양이 지면 회색으로 변하는 구름들이 이런건 강이 유유히 흘러간다, 구름이 오르락 내리락했다.
Ln. 5 lure   n. 매력
Ln. 9 gossamer   n. 아주 가는 거미줄
       swath   n. 면봉, 붕
       spectacle   n. 구경거리

6. THING: Contrasting Pair (Animal vs. Human perception)
Answer key: 이 질문은 "What can humans do that horses can't?"로 바꾸어 생각할 수 있다. "gossamer swath of Hale-Bopp" (line 9), "wondrous spectacle that is the night sky" (line 10)에서 볼 수 있듯이 author는 자연의 아름다움을 묘사하고 있다. (D)에서만 "nature's beauty"를 mention함으로 (D)가 답이다.

Key point Hale-Bopp, night sky = nature's beauty

Eliminate
(A) mistake는 not mentioned
(B) company of others는 not mentioned
(C) past experiences는 not mentioned
(E) simplicity는 not mentioned

특별히 CR이 600점대 이하의, 유학 3년차 이하의 학생들은 찍기 식으로 가르치는 학원보다는 지문을 잘 이해시켜 주는 curriculum을 제공하는 학원과 교재를 선정하여 공부하는 것이 좋다. 그리고 SAT는 미국대학에 진학하려는 학생을 위한 시험이므로, 평소에 미국적 사고에 필요한 역사, 문학, 사회이슈들에 대한 배경지식을 잘 정리해 놓으면 지문을 이해하고 문제풀이 시간을 줄이는데 도움이 된다.

B. Writing and Language Test (문법)

1. Real-world에 관한 지문
   - 역사/사회, 과학, 인문학, Career 관련 지문
   - 그래프, 도표 문제 한 개 이상 출제: 주어진 정보들을 어떻게 잘 연결해서 자연스럽고 논리적인 글로 만들어낼 수 있는가에 대한 문제 출제

2. 문법적 오류 관련문제는 크게 변화 없음
   - Development of idea
     예) adding relevant supporting details, improving focus and cohesion
   - Careful & purposeful use of words
     예) improving precision or concision
   - Rhetoricals and conventions
     예) fragments & run-ons, parallel structure, modifier, tense, pronoun & number, verb agreement, logical comparison, idiom, punctuation
   - Diction

3. 주어진 텍스트와 차트 또는 도표 간의 연관 찾기
   예) 차트에 대한 잘못된 해석 고치기

4. 지문 길이 증가
   - 기존의 한 문장 짜리 문법 문제 폐지
   - Extended context를 제공하는 문단 제공

> **학습전략**
>
> 기존 SAT Grammar 섹션에서 나오는 Improving Paragraph 유형에 Grammar 요소가 조금 더 가미되었다고 보면 된다. 너무 걱정하지 말고 조만간 출간될 Paul' SAT Writing and Language로 준비하면 된다. 아직 교재가 출간되지 않아 조바심이 나는 경우는 친절한 폴샘의 SAT Grammar 기본서로 공부를 해도 대부분 커버할 수 있으니 너무 걱정하지 말자.

C. Essay (에세이)

1. 요구사항에서 선택사항으로 변경

2. 짧게 자신의 의견을 요구하는 prompt 폐지
   - 기존의 prompt는 배경지식과 경험에 의존; 논리구조만 맞으면 fact는 상관 없었지만 새로운 SAT Essay에서는 600~700 단어로 주어진 글을 읽고 그 주장을 분석해서 설명해야 함 → 자기 마음대로 예시를 쓰거나, 단순히 자신의 주장을 펼치는 것이 아니라는 점에 주의
   예) 작가가 어떻게 주장을 이끌어 나가는지 텍스트 속 객관적 근거를 제시하여 설명하여야 하며, 자신의 의견은 쓰지 않음

- 글쓴이의 주장과 논리를 분석하여 그 논리전개에 대하여, 또한 그 주장에 대한 찬성 또는 반대의 관점을 어떻게 자기의 말로 잘 풀어내는지가 포인트

3. 채점방식 및 기준
   - 기존의 0~12점대의 scale은 폐지되고 criteria에 따른 점수로 0~24점까지 채점
   - Reading: Source text와 main idea에 대한 이해가 중요하며, 얼마나 디테일이 정확한지, 텍스트 속의 근거를 얼마나 잘 사용하는지 등이 중요한 포인트
   - Analysis: 주어진 과제를 얼마나 잘 이해했는지, 작가가 논거를 펼치며 사용한 각종 element가 얼마나 효과적인지, 그리고 자신의 주장에 대한 근거를 잘 제시하고 있는지 부분에 중점
   - Writing: Central claim 사용, 효과적인 organization과 progression이 되고 있는지, 문장구조가 varied한지, 정확한 뜻의 단어를 사용하는지, 그리고 consistent한 스타일과 톤을 유지하는지, 문법적인 오류는 없는지 등이 중점채점사항

4. 에세이 시간이 25분에서 50분으로 길어졌기 때문에, 체계적인 논리와 전개과정이 필수적이다. 시간이 길어지면서 그만큼 평가도 정확하고 가혹하게 될 것이라 예상된다.

> **학습전략**
>
> 기존 SAT는 내용을 '지어낼' 수 있었던 반면, Redesigned SAT는 fact-based essay이다. 2016 Redesigned Reading처럼 저자의 main idea와 argument를 잘 파악하여 fact-based argument를 하는 연습이 매우 중요해졌다. 이 연습만 잘 된다면 해외고 유학생들이 국내대학의 영어특기자 입시를 준비할 경우에 많은 도움이 될 것이다.

D. Math Test (수학)

*출제범위 및 비중이 조정되었기 때문에 일단 전반적으로 수학문제의 난이도가 올라가게 되며, 일부 문제는 AP 시험유형과 수준의 문제라고 생각하고 준비해야 한다.

1. Data Analysis에 중점
   - Reading과 Writing에서 Real-world에 중점을 둔 것과 같은 맥락
   - 실제 상황에 적용해서 푸는 문제들이 출제된다는 뜻

2. Real-world context 사용한 문제 출제
   예) 사회/역사/과학과 관련된 시나리오를 보여준 후 그것에 대한 문제 여러 개 출제

3. Pre-Calculus 영역이 추가됨
   - Trigonometry, Complex Number, Radians 등의 상급개념 추가

4. 일부 섹션에서 계산기 사용이 제한됨
   - 복잡한 계산은 아니고 유리수 산술계산 정도의 수준
   - Grid-ins 형태의 주관식이 총 12문제 출제

〈출제범위〉

범위	문제 개수	출제비중
Heart of Algebra (Creating, Solving, Interpreting Linear Expressions)	21	36%
Problem Solving and Data Analysis	16	27%
Passport to Advanced Math (Quadratic/Exponential Functions)	15	26%
Additional Topics (Area/Volume Calculation, Investigation of Lines, Angles, Triangles and Circles Using Theorem, Working with Trigonometric Functions)	6	11%
계	58	100%

〈계산기 사용에 따른 구분〉

구분	유형	시험시간
계산기 사용가능	객관식 30문제 Grid-ins 8문제	55분
계산기 사용불가	객관식 15문제 Grid-ins 5문제	25분
계	총 58문제	총 80분

> **학습전략**
>
> Pre-Calculus 영역을 중점 학습하고, 특히 trigonometry(삼각함수), complex number(복소수), radians(호도법) 등의 개념학습을 충실히 한다. 그리고 계산기를 사용할 수 없는 section이 하나 있으므로, 평소 계산연습을 많이 해 두도록 하고, real-world situation에 입각한 문제에 대비하기 위해 관련 응용문제 풀이를 많이 하도록 한다. 여름방학에 2016 SAT 학원수강을 하게 되면 꼭꼭 Math수업을 수강하여서 고득점의 발판을 마련하여야 한다. 더 이상 SAT 1 Math는 유학생들에게 쉬운 과목이 아니라는 점을 꼭 명심하도록 하자.

CONTENTS

Part 1_ Test 1 ·· 15
    Reading Test ··· 16
    English Test ·· 39
    Math Test (No Calculator) ·································· 47
    Math Test (Calculator) ·· 50

Part 2_ Test 2 ·· 57
    Reading Test ··· 58
    English Test ·· 82
    Math Test (No Calculator) ·································· 89
    Math Test (Calculator) ·· 92

Part 3_ Test 3 ·· 99
    Reading Test ··· 100
    English Test ·· 126
    Math Test (No Calculator) ·································· 134
    Math Test (Calculator) ·· 138

Part 4_ Test 4 ·· 145
    Reading Test ··· 146
    English Test ·· 171
    Math Test (No Calculator) ·································· 178
    Math Test (Calculator) ·· 181

Part 1

Practice Test #1

Part I

Practice Test #1

Section 1. Reading Test

Passage I. "The Strangeness of Beauty"

Passage Summary

Lines

- **1-4:** Akira might have been accepted as a suitor if he had followed tradition and sent a letter instead of showing up in person.
- **5-10:** He came during bad weather, so they didn't hear him at first, but then they let him in.
- **11-22:** Chie and her daughter Naomi are reading quietly together. Naomi recognizes Akira's name on the card and Chie goes to meet him.
- **23-52:** He greets Chie very formally, standing in the rain. Because of this she likes him at first, but has no idea why he is there. She is amused by him and thinks of him as a child. He is going to America to be a dentist there.
- **53-70:** She is shocked to discover that he wants to marry Naomi. She did not think of her daughter as a woman yet. Because he is from a lower family, he will join their family if Chie accepts. If not, he will take their daughter to America.
- **71-78:** He leaves and says he will give her two weeks to think about it. Chie is stunned and thinks of him as a thief.
- **79-95:** She expects Naomi to find his proposal ridiculous, but Naomi wants him too.

Main Idea

Akira comes to propose to Naomi in a non–traditional fashion. Her mother is surprised, but Naomi wants to marry him.

Tone

Neutral

Vocabulary

Line 4	receptive	a.	(새로운 사상, 제안에 대해) 수용적인
Line 5	pounded on	v.	~을 마구 내리쳤다
Line 6	shuttered	a.	셔터가 내려진
Line 8	scuttling	a.	종종걸음을 치는
Line 9	creak	n.	삐걱거리는 소리
Line 13	atop	prep.	꼭대기에, 맨 위에
Line 13	brazier	n.	화로, 난로
Line 15	tucked	v.	접어 넣은
Line 18	lacquer	n.	래커(광택제), 래커칠
Line 28	glistening	a.	반짝거리는, 번들거리는
Line 29	rain–drenched	a.	비로 흠뻑 젖은
Line 29	paving stone		(길바닥의) 포장용 돌, 포석
Line 31	disruption	n.	중단, 두절
Line 34	deferential	a.	경의를 표하는, 공손한
Line 34	peek	n.	(재빨리) 훔쳐봄
Line 37	nasty	a.	(아주 나빠서) 끔찍한, 형편없는
Line 50	endearingly	adv.	친밀감이 있게, 귀엽게
Line 57	blushed	a.	얼굴이 빨개졌다
Line 60	dampness	n.	축축(눅눅)함
Line 64	candidacy	n.	입후보, 출마
Line 64	unseemliness	n.	볼품없음, 꼴사나움
Line 65	go–between	n.	중개자
Line 72	abruptly	adv.	갑자기, 불쑥
Line 83	preposterous	a.	말도 안 되는, 터무니없는, 가당찮은
Line 86	in the snap of his fingers		손가락만 까딱하면
Line 87	ripe laughter		한바탕 웃음

Questions

Q1 THING: Main Idea

Answer Key : (B)

Akira가 Naomi의 어머니 Chie한테, 딸과 결혼하게 해 달라고 request하고 있다. Line 47에서 "had no idea," line 72–73에서 "I see I've startled you"를 보면 어머니 Chie는 전혀 예상하지 못한 request에 당황하고 있다.

Second best answer : (A)

Character 한 명이 다른 한 명의 집에 intrude하긴 하지만 argue하지 않고 서로 예의를 지키면서 얘기하고 있음

Eliminate

(A) argue하는 것은 아님

(C) 과거에 대해서 생각하는 게 아니라 미래에 대해서 고민하고 있음

(D) 같이 있을 때 직접 criticize하는 내용은 없었음

Q2 THING: Main Idea

Answer Key : (B)

Passage에서 detail들이 많이 나온다. 배경에 대한 detail (lines 5–6), character들의 목소리나 눈빛 등을 자세하게 describe하고 있다.

Second best answer : (C)

Akira와 Naomi가 결혼할 수 있는지에 대한 question은 definitive response 없이 끝남

Eliminate

(A) line 1–4에서 Akira의 청혼 방식은 tradition을 break한다고 되어 있음

(C) definitive response 없음

(D) Chie한테 Akira의 request는 cheerful/amusing이 아니라 startling

Q3 THING: Vocabulary

Answer Key : (C)

Line 1에서 "came directly, breaking all tradition"이라고 함 → mediation 없이 행동했다는 것을 의미한다.

Eliminate

(A), (B), (D) wrong meaning

Q4 THING: Point of View

Answer Key : (A)

Lines 63–64에 Akira가 Chie한테 "Please don't judge my candidacy by the unseemliness of this proposal"이라고 하면서 자기 proposal을 inappropriate하게 생각할까봐 걱정하고 있다.

Second best answer: (C)

갑작스러운 visit이 방해가 되었을까봐 걱정하기도 하지만, most fear하는 것은 아님

Eliminate

(B), (D) not mentioned

(C) most fear하지 않음

Q5 THING: Line Evidence

Answer Key : (C)

4번 문제의 답이 subject로 나오는 문장을 찾아보자. Lines 63–64에서 Akira가 Chie한테 자기 proposal을 unseemly하다고 생각해서 거절하지 말라고 부탁하고 있는 내용이 나온다.

Eliminate

(A), (B), (D) keywords가 not mentioned

Q6 THING: Main Idea

Answer Key : (D)

　Akira는 line 26에서 bow하고, line 31에서 "Madame"이라고 부르면서 계속 respect를 보여주고 있다. 하지만, tradition에 따르지 않더라도 Naomi와 꼭 결혼하고 싶다고 자기 의사를 강조하기 때문에 utter deference는 아니다.

Eliminate

　(A) respect는 보이지만, affection을 보여주는 line은 없음

　(B), (C) not mentioned

Q7 THING: Main Idea

Answer Key : (D)

　Lines 1-4에서 narrator는 Akira가 더 traditional한 방법으로 청혼했으면 Chie가 받아줬을지 질문한다. 그러므로 첫 문단의 purpose는 Chie가 왜 그런 반응을 보였는지 examine하는 것이다.

Eliminate:

　(A) Japanese culture 중에서 청혼의 culture만 describe하지, 전체 culture를 describe하지 않음

　(B) Akira의 청혼에 대해서 criticize한다고 볼 수도 있지만, Japanese tradition 자체를 criticize하는 내용은 없음

　(C) not mentioned

Q8 THING: Vocabulary

Answer Key : (B)

　Line 1에서 Akira가 tradition을 break했다고 함 → "form"은 tradition을 의미한다.

Eliminate

　(A), (C), (D) wrong meaning in context

Q9 THING: Main Idea, Problem

Answer Key : (C)

　Lines 41-42에서 dentist가 되기 위해 미국으로 가야 한다고 말한다.

Second best answer: (D)

　Chie가 Akira의 감정을 모르고 있었다는 것은 맞지만, urgency에 대한 내용이 누락됨

Eliminate

　(A) Akira가 자기 부모님에 대해서 걱정하는 것은 아님

　(B) line 63에서 Akira와 Naomi 사이에 "understanding"이 있다고 함

　(D) urgency에 대한 내용이 누락됨

Q10 THING: Line Evidence

Answer Key : (B)

9번 문제의 답인 "attractive job in another country"가 subject로 등장하는 lines를 찾아보자. Lines 39–42 에서 Akira가 미국에 있는 job에 대해서 얘기하고 있다.

Eliminate

(A), (C), (D) 미국에 있는 job에 대한 내용이 subject로 나오지 않음

Passage II. "Money Can't Buy Love"

Passage Summary

Lines

1-16: People give a lot of gifts. Some enjoy it, some don't.

17-34: People buy gifts for others that others wouldn't buy themselves, and they spend more money on them. They are also bad at predicting what people might want.

35-50: This is strange since everyone has experience at both buying and receiving gifts. The author argues that people assume that how much they spend will be how much they are appreciated, but that in fact this is not true.

51-65: Since gift giving is seen as a kind of ritual, gift givers think that more money spent signals more respect and appreciation, even though the receiver might not pick this up.

66-81: It is hard to believe that we don't understand this when buying a present, because we all fill both these roles all the time.

Main Idea

While many exchange gifts because they want to create a stronger bond with their friends, that assumption is probably not true according to psychological research.

Tone

Informative, questioning

Vocabulary

Line 3	frantically	*adv.*	미친 듯이, 극도로 흥분하여
Line 10	engender	*v.*	(어떤 감정, 상황을) 낳다, 불러일으키다
Line 10	ambivalent	*a.*	반대 감정이 병존하는, 애증이 엇갈리는
Line 11	relish	*v.*	(어떤 것을 대단히) 즐기다, 좋아하다
Line 14	dread	*a.*	(~을) 몹시 무서워하다; (안 좋은 일이 생길까 봐) 두려워하다
Line 16	recipient	*n.*	(어떤 것을) 받는 사람, 수취인
Line 20	favorable	*a.*	호의적인, 호의를 보이는; 찬성하는
Line 24	phenomenon	*n.*	현상
Line 25	deadweight	*a.*	(자체적으로 움직이지 않는, 대단히 무거운 것의) 무게
Line 25	to wit		더 정확히 말해서

Line 33	egocentrism	n.	자기 중심(성)
Line 41	equate	v.	동일시하다
Line 46	intuitive	a.	생각이 직감(직관)에 의한
Line 47	unfounded	a.	근거 없는, 사실 무근의
Line 49	magnitude	v.	(엄청난) 규모, 중요도
Line 63	construe	v.	~을 (~으로) 이해, 해석하다
Line 68	slip	v.	미끄러지다; (옷 등을) 재빨리 입다
Line 80	calibrate	v.	(계기 등에) 눈금을 매기다
Line 81	expenditure	n.	(공공 기금의) 지출, 비용, 경비

Questions

Q11 THING: Main Idea, List

Answer Key : (A)

Lines 1–9에서 사람들이 "regularly" 기념일을 위해 shopping한다는 내용이다. 즉, 1년 동안 얼마나 규칙적으로 shopping하는지 알 수 있다.

Second best answer: (D)

Lines 1–9에서 기념일들이 mention되지만, 기념일의 수가 focus는 아님

Eliminate

(B), (C), (D) lines 1–9의 focus가 아님

Q12 THING: Vocabulary

Answer Key : (B)

Lines 11–15를 보면, gift-giver들이 gift를 주는 것을 "relish"하는 동시에 "dread"하고 "worry"한다고 한다. 즉, conflicted한 feelings를 가지고 있다.

Eliminate

(A), (C), (D) wrong meaning

Q13 THING: Point of View

Answer Key : (D)

Lines 10–13에서 선물을 주는 것은 "build stronger bonds"할 수 있는 기회라고 한다. 즉 relationship을 strengthen할 수 있다.

Second best answer: (B)

Appreciation을 보여주는 것으로 사용되지만, inexpensive하지 않음

Eliminate

(A), (B), (C) self-expression / inexpensive / required는 not mentioned

Q14 THING: Line Evidence

Answer Key : (A)

13번 문제의 keyword인 "strengthen a relationship"이 나오는 lines를 찾아보자. Lines 10–13에서 선물을 통해서 "stronger bonds"를 만들 수 있다고 한다.

Eliminate

(B), (C), (D) keyword나 synonym of keywords가 not mentioned

Q15 THING: Point of View

Answer Key : (A)

Lines 31–34에서 social psychologists들은 이미 사람들은 서로 다른 perspective를 잘 이해하지 못하는 것을 안다고 나와있다. 즉 deadweight loss도 predictable하게 생각할 것이다.

Eliminate

(B), (C), (D) question, disturbed, surprised는 not mentioned

Q16 THING: Point of View, Problem

Answer Key : (C)

Lines 41–44에서 gift-giver들은 선물이 costly할수록 더 appreciated될 것이라고 생각한다. 하지만 line 47에서는 그런 생각이 "unfounded"하다고 말하고 있다. → context 상 unfounded = incorrect.

Eliminate

(A), (B), (D) insincere, unreasonable, substantiated는 not mentioned

Q17 THING: Line Evidence

Answer Key : (C)

16번 문제의 답인 "the assumption made by gift-givers" (선물 cost = 받는 사람의 appreciation) 이 "incorrect"하다는 내용의 subject를 가진 lines를 찾아보자. Lines 63–65에서 "may not construe smaller and larger gifts as representing smaller and larger signals of thoughtfulness"라고 말하면서, "선물 cost = 받는 사람 appreciation"이 틀렸다는 것을 suggest하고 있다.

Eliminate

(A), (B), (D) "assumption made by gift-givers"가 subject로 나오지 않음

Q18 THING: Vocabulary

Answer Key : (D)

Lines 53–55에서 "gifts convey stronger signals"라고 함 → context 상 signals를 "convey"한다는 것은 communicate를 의미한다.

Eliminate

(A), (B), (C) wrong meaning in context

Q19 THING: Point of View

Answer Key : (A)

Camerer는 선물을 주는 사람들의 reasoning을 설명함: "gift-givers ... signal their positive attitudes ... and their willingness to invest resources in a future relationship" (lines 57–60).

Eliminate

(B), (C) argument를 제시/question하기보다는 생각을 explain하려고 함

(D) conclusion이 아님

Q20 THING: Graph

Answer Key : (B)

Graph에서 선물을 주는 사람들은 valuable 선물은 더 appreciate될 것이라고 생각한다는 것을 보여준다.

Eliminate

(A) graph에서 선물 주는 사람들이 선물 받는 사람들이 얼마나 appreciate하는지에 대해서 알고 있다는 내용은 not mentioned

(C), (D) 자기가 산 선물에 대한 desire나 선물 주는 사람과 받는 사람의 relationship은 관계에서 not mentioned

Q21 THING: Main Idea

Answer Key : (A)

Lines 70–75에서 대부분의 사람들은 선물을 주고 받은 experience를 모두 갖고 있지만, 그 experience를 통해서 입장을 바꿔 생각하자는 내용이다.

Eliminate

(B), (C) not mentioned

(D) 서로 intention을 이해하지 못하는 것은 mentioned, 하지만 그것이 difference of appreciation의 가장 큰 이유가 된다는 것은 not mentioned

Passage III. "Genetical Implications ..."

Passage Summary

Lines

1-11: We are confident that DNA is a long chain of chemicals. Purines: adenine and guanine, and Pyrimidines: thymine and cytosine. They bond together to make DNA.

12-19: We thought there was only one axis in the structure since the chemical formula is one chain, but it looks like there are actually two axes instead.

20-30: Hydrogen bonds bind the bases together, and only certain pairs of bonds will work. One must be a purine and the other a pyrimidine to link them.

31-38: Because of this, there are only a few possible base pairs of purines and pyrimidines.

39-end: The phosphate sugar base can hold any combination of these pairs. Since every chemical has a set pair, it is possible to predict the other chemical in the set, and this explains how DNA duplicates itself.

Main Idea

Since the structure and chemical makeup of DNA can be predicted, we can understand how it might duplicate itself.

Tone

Informative, straightforward

Vocabulary

Line 1	deoxyribonucleic	*a.*	디옥시리보핵산의
Line 2	molecule	*n.*	(화학) 분자
Line 3	backbone	*n.*	척추, 등뼈
Line 4	alternation	*n.*	교대, 교체; 하나씩 거름
Line 4	phosphate	*n.*	인산염
Line 5	nitrogenous	*a.*	질소의[를 함유한]
Line 7	adenine	*n.*	아데닌 (췌장 등 조직 또는 찻잎에 있는 푸린 염기)
Line 7	guanine	*n.*	구아닌 (DNA, RNA를 구성하는 퓨린 염기의 하나)
Line 7	purine	*n.*	푸린 (요산 화합물의 원질)
Line 8	thymine	*n.*	티민 (DNA를 구성하는 염기의 하나)
Line 8	cytosine	*n.*	시토신 (핵산의 중요성분)

Line 8	pyrimidine	n.	피리미딘 (마취성의 자극적 냄새가 나는 결정체)
Line 10	monomer	n.	단량체, 모노머 (cf. polymer, 폴리머)
Line 11	nucleotide	n.	뉴클레오티드 (핵산의 구성성분)
Line 14	coiled around		도르르 감겼다
Line 34	restrictive	a.	(자유 등을) 제한[구속]하는
Line 42	permutation	n.	순열, 치환
Table	maize	n.	(영국식) 옥수수
Table	sea urchin	n.	성게

Questions

Q22 THING: Main Idea

Answer Key : (B)

Lines 2–4에서 DNA는 "long chain, the backbone of which consists of a regular alternation of sugar and phosphate groups"라고 했다. Regular alternation은 repeating units와 뜻이 비슷하고, DNA chain의 structure임을 알 수 있다.

Eliminate

(A) spinal column of organisms는 not mentioned

(C) passage에서 말한 "regular alternation"과 "consists entirely of"는 서로 다른 뜻

(D) nitrogenous bases는 DNA의 main structure가 아니라 sugar에만 붙어있음

Q23 THING: Main Idea, Contrasting Pairs

Answer Key : (D)

Nitrogenous bases가 pair할 때 "One member of a pair must be a purine and the other a pyrimidine in order to bridge between the two chains"라고 한다(lines 27–29) → random한 것이 아니라 정해진 rules가 있다는 것을 알 수 있다.

Eliminate

(A), (B), (C) nitrogenous bases가 random하게 pair한다는 student's claim과 관련 없는 내용

Q24 THING: Main Idea

Answer Key : (D)

Lines 12–14에서 "the first feature of our structure which is of biological interest is that it consists not of one chain, but of two"라고 했다. 즉 biological interest인 것은 DNA가 chain이 2개 있다는 것이다.

Eliminate

(A), (B) "biological interest"가 된다는 내용은 없음

(C) DNA chain이 2개인 것을 아는데 X-ray가 도움이 되었지만, 그것이 biological interest는 아니었음

Q25 THING: Main Idea, Point of View

Answer Key : (C)

Lines 18–19에서 "the density, taken with the X-ray evidence, suggests very strongly that there are two [chains]"라고 했다. 즉 X-ray evidence와 density를 mention하는 가장 큰 purpose는 DNA chain이 2개 있다는 것을 support하기 위함이다.

Eliminate

(A), (B), (D) "DNA carries genetic information, hypothesis about composition of a nucleotide, relationship between density and chemical formula of DNA"는 not mentioned

Q26 THING: Main Idea

Answer Key : (B)

Lines 25–26에서 "only certain pairs of bases will fit into the structure"라고 했다. 즉 purine과 pyrimidine이 pair되지 않고 purine 2개가 pair되면 너무 커서 fit into하지 못할 것이다.

Eliminate

(A), (C), (D) distance between sugar & phosphate group, pyrimidines와 purines 크기 비교, pyrimidines와 purine–pyrimidine pair의 크기 비교는 not mentioned

Q27 THING: Tone, Point of View

Answer Key : (D)

Bases들의 순서를 알면 다른 chain에 있는 bases의 순서도 알 수 있다. "If the actual order ... were given, one could write down the exact order of the bases on the other one" (lines 45–46). 즉 "exact", "specific", "complement" 등의 단어들은 DNA chain이 predictable한 template이라는 것을 보여준다.

Eliminate

(A) most nucleotide sequences are known에 대한 내용은 not mentioned
(B) 주어진 lines에서는 base sequence가 random하다고 discuss하지 않음
(C) 주어진 lines에서는 sugar에 붙어있는 bases만 discuss하고 있음

Q28 THING: Graph

Answer Key : (C)

그래프에서는 adenine과 guanine이 31.3%와 18.7%로 되어 있다.

Eliminate

(A), (B), (D) not supported by the graph

Q29 THING: Graph

Answer Key : (A)

Lines 34–35에서 "the only pairs of bases possible are: adenine with thymine, and guanine with cytosine"이라고 함. Table을 보면 adenine과 thymine의 %가 비슷하고, guanine과 cytosine의 %가 비슷하다는 것을 알 수 있다.

Second best answer: (B)

Yes는 맞지만, explanation이 그래프와 맞지 않음

Eliminate

(C), (D) 지문에서 나왔던 pairs를 support하지 않음

Q30 THING: Graph

Answer Key : (A)

Line 35에서 "adenine with thymine, and guanine with cytosine"이라고 pair한 것과 가장 잘 맞는다. Cytosine이 17.3%이고, guanine은 17.7%이다.

Eliminate

(B), (C), (D) table의 data와 맞지 않음

Q31 THING: Graph

Answer Key : (D)

Table을 보면 adenine이 각 organism의 DNA에 따라 다르다는 것을 알 수 있다. Lines 41–43에서 "in a long molecule many different permutations are possible"이라고 말하면서 이렇게 다양할 수 있다는 것을 보여준다.

Eliminate

(A), (B) not supported by the table

(C) variability에 대한 내용 not mentioned

Passage IV. "Three Guineas"

Passage Summary

Lines

1-11: Let us stand on a bridge over River Thames, a good place to look over London as a whole, and consider an important issue: gender equality.

12-24: Men have been much more educated than women in the past, but now women have started to become educated themselves.

24-45: I think women will soon become great leaders in society, and I urge other women to share my hopes.

45-59: I ask a question which is very important for both men and women but needs quick action—do we want gender equality our (women's) way, or their (men's) way?

59-end: We must question ourselves constantly whether we want our own system or we may just follow the men's system.

Main Idea

The author dreams of an era of powerful women but asks fellow women to think about how that will happen.

Tone

Persuasive, passionate, poetic

Vocabulary

Line 2	vantage	n.	우세, 유리
Line 3	barge	n.	바지선[너벅선] (운하, 강 등에서 사람, 화물을 싣고 다니는, 바닥이 납작한 배)
Line 3	laden		(~을) 잔뜩 실은
Line 6	parliament	n.	의회, 국회
Line 10	procession	n.	(특히 의식의 일부로 하는) 행진, 행렬
Line 15	pulpit	n.	(교회의) 설교단[연단]
Line 17	transacting	a.	거래하는
Line 18	caravanserai	n.	(과거 아시아, 북부 아프리카 사막에 있던) 여행자 쉼터[숙소]
Line 21	fresco	n.	프레스코화[화법] (새로 석회를 바른 벽에 그것이 마르기 전에 그림을 그리는 것)

Line 22	esthetic	n.	심미적인, 미학적인, 미적인, 미를 살려 만든 (=aesthetic)
Line 23	trapese	v.	traipse의 old form. 터벅터벅(느릿느릿) 걷다
Line 26	pageant	n.	(역사적 내용을 다룬) 야외극; 가장 행렬
Line 32	administer	v.	(회사, 조직, 국가 등을) 관리하다[운영하다]
Line 32	agitate	v.	(특히 법적, 사회적 사항 등의 변경을 강력히) 주장하다[요구하다]
Line 40	coal-scuttle	n.	(난로 옆에 두는) 석탄통
Line 41	plume	n.	(연기, 수증기 등이 피어오르는) 기둥
Line 41	venerable	a.	숭고한, 존엄스러운
Line 51	transition	n.	(다른 상태, 조건으로의) 이행[과도]
Line 61	bazaar	n.	(일부 동양 국가들에서) 상점가[시장 거리]
Line 67	cloister	n.	(보통 성당, 수도원의 지붕이 덮인) 회랑
Line 67	seclude	v.	(다른 사람들로부터) 은둔하다, 고립시키다
Line 68	rock	v.	(전후, 좌우로 부드럽게) 흔들리다[흔들다]
Line 72	omnibus	n.	옴니버스 (최근 텔레비전, 라디오 프로 몇 개를 시리즈로 묶은 것)

Questions

Q32 THING: Main Idea, Tone

Answer Key : (B)

Lines 48-49에서 Woolf는 women에게 "very little time"이 있다고 강조한다 → urgency를 stress하고 있다.

Eliminate

(A) tradition을 emphasize하는 것이 아니라 criticize하고 있음

(C) severity of social divisions를 강조하기 보다는 그런 divisions가 줄어들 수 있다고 add함

(D) feasibility를 question하는 것이 아니라 change하자고 urge하고 있음

Q33 THING: Main Idea

Answer Key : (A)

Lines 30-32에서 "we too can leave the house, can mount those steps ... make money, administer justice"라고 하면서 여자들에게 join the workforce하자고 urge함 → existing institution과 engage하는 방법이다.

Eliminate

(B) tradition에 대해서 discuss하지만, important position을 가지기 위해서 모든 tradition을 포기해야 한다는 말은 없음

(C) male monopoly를 describe하지만, grave and continuing effects는 not mentioned

(D) changing the workforce dynamic은 not mentioned

Q34 THING: Tone

Answer Key : (C)

"We"를 계속 사용하면서 solidarity를 강조한다.

Eliminate

(A), (D) Woolf가 원하는 것은 solidarity among women

(B) thinking을 traditional role에서 했다고 말하지만, "we"와는 관련 없음

Q35 THING: Main Idea, List

Answer Key : (B)

Lines 1–3에서 "bridge … [has] an admirable vantage ground for us to make a survey"라고 했다. Make a survey는 여기서 뭔가를 carefully 보는 것을 말한다. 그러므로 good view를 준다는 이유로 bridge를 setting으로 정한 것이다.

Eliminate

(A) line 6–9에서 "consider the facts"한다고 되어 있으니까 그저 fanciful dreaming만 하는 것은 아님

(C), (D) historic episodes, symbol of male–dominated past는 not mentioned

Q36 THING: Main Idea

Answer Key : (D)

Lines 23–24에서 "at the tail end of the procession, we go ourselves"하면서 recently 여자들도 work하기 시작하고 있다고 했다.

Eliminate

(A) procession은 옛날부터 influential했음

(B), (C) not mentioned

Q37 THING: Line Evidence

Answer Key : (C)

36번 문제 답의 keywords인 "procession", "less exclusionary"가 나오는 lines를 찾아보자. Lines 23–24에서 여자들도 남자들만 있었던 procession에 join한다는 비유는 procession이 "less exclusionary" 해졌다는 것을 imply하고 있다.

Eliminate

(A), (B), (D) keywords나 keywords의 synonym이 나오지 않음

Q38 THING: Question, Tone

Answer Key : (D)

Lines 52–53에서 question들이 "so important they may well change the lives of all men and women for ever"라고 하면서 significance를 강조하고 있다.

Eliminate

(A) controversy or fear는 not mentioned

(B) question들이 "important"하긴 하지만, answer할 수 있다고 imply함
(C) question들이 mysterious하다고 imply하지 않음

Q39 THING: Line Evidence

Answer Key : (B)

38번 문제에 대한 답의 keywords인 "momentous", "pressing"이 나오는 lines를 찾아보자. Lines 48-49에서 keywords의 synonym으로, questions가 "important"하다고 강조하고 "very little time"이 있다고 말하면서 urgency를 보여주고 있다.

Eliminate

(A), (C), (D) keywords가 나오지 않음

Q40 THING: Main Idea

Answer Key : (C)

여기서 "sixpence"는 사전적 의미가 아니라, 여자들이 workforce로 들어가는 opportunity를 비유한 표현이다.

Eliminate

(A), (B), (D) wrong meaning in context

Q41 THING: Main Idea, List

Answer Key : (B)

Lines 72-76에서 계속 "Let us think"라고 계속 말하면서 여자들이 자기 role in society에 대해서 think하는 것의 중요성을 emphasize하고 있다.

Eliminate

(A), (C), (D) passage에서 emphasize한 내용이 아님

Passage V. "Space Mining" / "Taming the Final Frontier"

Passage 1

Passage Summary

Lines

- **1-8:** A recent convention in Sydney claimed that there is money to be made from space mining.
- **9-17:** There are a number of new companies that want to mine in space.
- **18-28:** They want to make money mining rare earth minerals, but they don't want to just make money on Earth. They want to build manufacturing in space for future space missions.
- **29-34:** Water will be one of the most valuable things in space to mine.
- **35-40:** Water mined from the moon could be sent for use at the international space station.
- **41-end:** Other materials could be turned into other useful things.

Main Idea

Space Mining could be useful for Space Exploration

Tone

Informative, speculative, eager

Passage 2

Passage Summary

Lines

- **46-52:** Many people are talking about the money to be made from mining in space, but everyone will benefit from it.
- **46-52:** Many people are talking about the money to be made from mining in space, but everyone will benefit from it.
- **54-59:** But before we get started, we need to think about the consequences.
- **60-66:** Some would say we shouldn't ruin space or put more stuff on earth.
- **67-72:** However, this is probably not enough to convince people to stop space mining, since space is huge and far away.

73-78: Regardless, we may need the resources in space more than on Earth. Also, there are no laws for space mining yet.

79-end: The miners themselves want to avoid regulation, but laws will help people resolve disputes, so we should establish some.

Main Idea

Space Mining needs to establish some ground rules before it gets started.

Tone

Helpful, thoughtful

Vocabulary

Line 2	first-of-its-kind	a.	그 종류의 첫 번째의
Line 4	convene	v.	(회의 등을) 소집하다
Line 6	robotics	n.	로봇 공학
Line 10	unveiling	n.	(기념비 등의 제막식)
Line 10	asteroid	n.	소행성
Line 12	prospecting	n.	탐사(탐광)
Line 20	platinum	n.	백금
Line 20	vital	a.	필수적인
Line 21	yttrium	n.	이트륨 (희토류 원소의 하나)
Line 22	lanthanum	n.	란타늄 (희토류의 금속 원소)
Line 25	off-planet	a.	지구와 동떨어진, 지구와 별개의
Line 30	commodity	n.	상품, 물품; 원자재
Line 37	radiation	n.	방사선
Line 39	interplanetary	a.	행성 간의
Line 41	eye	v.	(특히 탐이 나거나 의심스러워서) 쳐다보다
Line 48	flurry	n.	일진광풍, 질풍, 강풍, 돌풍
Line 48	celestial	a.	하늘의, 천체의, 천상의
Line 51	bounty	n.	너그러움, 풍부함
Line 51	spin-off	a.	파생효과, 파생상품
Line 55	sidestep	v.	(대답, 문제 처리를) 회피하다
Line 61	desolation	n.	고적감
Line 62	despoil	v.	(어떤 장소에서 귀중한 것을) 빼앗다[훼손하다]
Line 63	pristine	n.	완전 새 것 같은, 아주 깨끗한

Line 64	glutting	n.	과잉공급 (← glut)
Line 65	sustainable	a.	(환경 파괴 없이) 지속 가능한
Line 69	barren	a.	(땅, 토양이) 척박한, 황량한
Line 73	off-world	a.	(이) 세상과(지구와) 동떨어진, 별개의
Line 74	orbit	n.	궤도
Line 76	stewardship	n.	(재산, 조직체 등의) 관리
Line 77	broach	v.	(하기 힘든 이야기를) 꺼내다
Line 77	regulatory	a.	(산업, 상업 분야의) 규제[단속]력을 지닌
Line 78	fragmentary	a.	단편적인, 부분의
Line 80	engage with	v.	~와 맞물리게 하다
Line 82	plea	n.	애원, 간청
Line 84	for-profit	a.	(공공기관, 병원 등이) 영리 목적의, 이익을 추구하는
Line 85	exploitation	n.	착취; 개발; (부당한) 이용
Line 85	consensus	n.	의견 일치, 합의
Line 86	dispute	v.	반박하다, 이의를 제기하다
Line 87	insecure	a.	(자기 자신에 대해서나 다른 사람과의 관계에 대해) 자신이 없는

Questions

Q42 THING: Main Idea, List

Answer Key : (B)

"Planetary Resources of Washington," "Deep Space Industries of Virginia," 그리고 "Golden Spike of Colorado" 같이 구체적인 companies를 mention하면서 많은 group들이 space mining을 현실로 만들려고 노력하고 있다는 것을 support하고 있다.

Eliminate

(A), (C), (D) technological advances, profit margins, diverse approaches에 관한 내용 not mentioned

Q43 THING: Main Idea, List

Answer Key : (A)

Lines 18-22에서 "[space mining] may be meeting earthly demands for precious metals ... and the rare earth elements"라고 했다. 그러므로 space mining의 장점 중 하나는 precious metals와 earth elements를 구할 수 있다는 것이다.

Eliminate

(B), (C), (D) "metals more valuable on Earth, unanticipated technological innovations, change scientists' understanding of space resources"는 not mentioned

Q44 THING: Line Evidence

Answer Key : (A)

43번 문제에 대한 답의 keywords인 "materials", "Earth's economy"가 등장하는 lines를 찾아보자. Lines 18–22에서 keywords의 synonym인, space mining을 통해 얻을 수 있는 "metals"와 "earthly demands"가 나온다.

Eliminate

(B), (C), (D): keywords가 나오지 않음

Q45 THING: Vocabulary

Answer Key : (D)

Lines 19–22에서 "earthly demands for precious metals ... and the rare earth elements"이라고 함. → "earthly demands"는 사람들이 precious metals와 rare earth elements를 want/desire하고 있다는 것을 뜻한다.

Eliminate

(A), (B), (C) wrong meaning in context

Q46 THING: Main Idea

Answer Key : (C)

Lines 29–30에서 "water mined from other worlds could become the most desired commodity"라고 얘기하며, lines 35–40에서 그런 물이 쓰일 수 있는 여러가지 방식을 보여주면서 hypothetical examples를 주고 있다.

Eliminate

(A) comparison을 extend하지는 않았음

(B) previous paragraph에 있었던 질문에 대한 답도 previous paragraph에 있었음

(D) previous paragraph에서 구체적인 proposal을 제시하기보다는 assertion과 question을 하나씩 했음

Q47 THING: Main Idea, Contrasting Pairs

Answer Key : (B)

Lines 50–52에서 "we all stand to gain: the mineral bounty and spin-off technologies could enrich us all"이라고 하면서 space mining이 인간에게 도움이 될 수 있다는 것을 보여주고 있다. 하지만 lines 57–59에서 "consequences – both here on Earth and in space – merit careful consideration"이라고 말하면서 조심해야 할 것을 말해주고 있다.

Second best answer: (A)

Lines 55–56에서 "space mining seems to sidestep ... environmental concerns"이라고 하지만, environment를 많이 harm할 것이라고 직접 말하지는 않음

Eliminate

(A) environment를 harm할 것이라고 직접 나오지는 않음

(C) not mentioned

(D) lines 74–76에서 "resources that are valuable in orbit and beyond may be very different to those we prize on Earth"라고 말하지만, space mining의 economically 좋은 점에 대한 disagreement를 보여주지 않음.

Q48 THING: Vocabulary

Answer Key : (A)

Lines 60–66: economical benefits들과 비교하면 environmental arguments를 "hold"하기 힘들 것이라고 함 → context 상 "hold"는 maintain을 의미한다.

Eliminate

(B), (C), (D) incorrect in context

Q49 THING: Point of View, Contrasting Pair

Answer Key : (D)

Passage 1에서는 space mining의 가능성을 보면서 excited해 있지만, Passage 2에서는 space mining이 benefit도 있을 수도 있지만 조심스럽게 해야 한다고 주장한다. 그러므로 Passage 2에서는 Passage 1에서 나온 concept에 대해서 concern을 보이고 있다.

Eliminate

(A) passage 2가 Passage 1을 refute하고 있지 않음. 둘 다 space mining에 좋은 점이 있을 수도 있음을 인정

(B) passage 1이 더 general한 term을 쓰지 않음

(C) passage 2에서 mining proposal이 impractical하다는 suggestion 없음

Q50 THING: Point of View, Contrasting Pair

Answer Key : (B)

Passage 2, lines 83–87에서 "miners have much to gain from a broad agreement … without consensus, claims will be disputed, investments risky, and the gains made insecure"라고 한다. 즉 regulation과 agreement 없이는 위험하다고 말하고 있다.

Eliminate

(A), (C), (D) space mining의 benefit이 unsustainable, unacheivable, negatively affect Earth's economy한다는 내용 not mentioned

Q51 THING: Line Evidence

Answer Key : (D)

50번 문제의 keyword인 "future of space mining"이 subject 로 나오는 lines를 찾아보자. Lines 83-87에서 "without consensus, claims will be disputed", "in all of our long-term interests" 등 future를 imply하는 phrase들이 나온다.

Eliminate

(A), (B), (C) keywords가 subject 아님

Q52 THING: Point of View

Answer Key : (A)

Passage 1과 Passage 2에서 둘 다 지구에서 valuable한 resources들이 space에서 제일 valuable한 resources와 다를 수 있다고 agree한다. Lines 25-30에서 space에서 mine된 water는 metals보다 중요할 수 있다고 말하고, lines 74-76에서도 "The resources that are valuable in orbit and beyond may be very different to those we prize on Earth"이라고 말한다.

Eliminate

(B) not mentioned

(C) passage 1에서만 mentioned

(D) passage 2에서 not mentioned

Section 2. Writing and Language Test

Q1
Answer : (D)
Category : Vocabulary
Explanation
문장의 context 상 Greek yogurt의 advantages가 drawbacks 보다 "비중이 크다, 중요하다"는 뜻의 단어 "outweigh"가 들어가야 한다. 정답은 (D)
Eliminate
(A), (C) "능가하다" 라는 뜻
(B) "전쟁에서 상대방을 패배시키다" 라는 뜻

Q2
Answer : (B)
Category : Insert/Delete/Replace
Explanation
Paragraph의 context를 살펴보자. 이 paragraph의 main idea는 Greek yogurt를 만들 때 environmental problem이 생긴다는 것이고, 이 문장에서는 그런 problem을 해결하기 위해 farmer들이 무엇을 하는지 설명하고 있다. Environmental problem과 관련된 문장은 (B)
Eliminate
(A), (C), (D) environmental problem과 관련 없음

Q3
Answer : (A)
Category : Tense Context, Apostrophes
Explanation
문장의 dependent clause에서 be verb의 present tense인 "is" 가 쓰였으므로, 뒤에도 "can"의 present tense인 "can"이 쓰여야 한다. 정답은 (A)
Eliminate
(B) "waterway"의 plural form인 "waterways"에는 apostrophe를 쓸 수 없음
(C), (D) "can"의 present tense가 쓰이지 않음

Q4
Answer : (C)
Category : Various Comma Usages
Explanation
문장에서 nouns를 list하고 있음. 각 noun 사이에는 comma가 있어야 하지만, "and" 다음에는 없어야 한다. 정답은 (C)
Eliminate
(A), (B) simple noun을 list 할 때는 semi-colon이나 colon 이 아닌 comma를 써야 함
(D) "and" 뒤에 comma 쓰지 않음

Q5
Answer : (C)
Category : Content Order
Explanation
Paragraph와 sentence 5의 content와 context를 잘 살펴보자. Sentence 5에서는 "it" (="acid whey") 을 improper 하게 "introduce into the environment", 즉 dispose하면 생길 수 있는 문제들을 자세히 설명한다. 그러므로 paragraph 내에서 acid whey를 dispose하기 어렵다는 내용의 문장 뒤에 와야 한다. 정답은 (C)
Eliminate
(A), (B), (D) 문단의 logical flow에 방해됨

Q6

Answer : (D)

Category : Insert/Delete/Replace

Explanation

   Paragraph와 underlined sentence의 content와 context를 잘 살펴보자. 이전까지 passage는 Greek yogurt가 environmental problem을 발생시키지 않도록 하기 위한 conservation methods에 대한 내용이었음. 하지만 이 paragraph의 main idea는 Greek yogurt가 여러 health benefit 들이 있다는 것이다. 그러므로 underlined sentence를 통한 transition이 꼭 필요하다. 정답은 (D)

Eliminate

   (A), (B) 이 문장은 transition을 위해 꼭 필요함

   (C) underlined sentence에는 how acid whey can be disposed of safely에 대한 내용 없음

Q7

Answer : (B)

Category : Idioms

Explanation

   "serves as"가 correct idiomatic expression이다. 정답은 (B)

Eliminate

   (A), (C), (D) correct idiomatic expression이 아님

Q8

Answer : (C)

Category : Parallelism

Explanation

   앞의 verb "is", "serves" 와 parallel 한 form이 쓰여야 한다. 정답은 (C)

Eliminate

   (A), (B), (D) 앞의 phrase/verb 들과 parallel하지 않음

Q9

Answer : (A)

Category : Vocabulary

Explanation

   Paragraph 내에서 나온 Greek yogurt의 health benefit을 하나 더 설명하는 문장이므로, additional information을 나타내는 conjunctive adverb가 나와야 함. 정답은 (A)

Eliminate

   (B), (C), (D) additional information을 나타내는 conjunctive adverb가 아님

Q10

Answer : (A)

Category : Vocabulary

Explanation

   Greek yogurt는 사람들이 더 오랫동안 "배가 부르게" 해 준다는 내용이므로, "satiated"가 쓰여야 한다. 정답은 (A)

Eliminate

   (B) "성취감을 느끼는"이라는 뜻

   (C) "자기만족적인"이라는 뜻

   (D) "충분한"이라는 뜻

Q11

Answer : (B)

Category : Conjunction Errors - Adverb Clause

Explanation

   "Because consumers reap . . . and sell it"은 뒤의 main clause를 modify 하는 adverb clause다. Comma 뒤에 바로 main clause가 나오면 된다. 정답은 (B)

Eliminate

   (A), (C) main clause 전에 "therefore", "so" 등의 conjunctive adverb 쓸 수 없음

   (D) semi-colon을 쓰면 앞의 adverb clause가 sentence fragment가 됨

Q12

Answer : (B)

Category : Graph

Explanation

Average daily high temperature가 제일 낮을 때 20 degrees 까지 내려가지만, 질문에서는 average daily low temperature를 묻고 있다. Average daily low temperature가 제일 낮았을 때는 May 5 조금 이후에 12 degrees였을 때였다. 정답은 (B)

Eliminate

(A), (C), (D) graph의 내용과 맞지 않음

Q13

Answer : (A)

Category : Back Modifier

Explanation

두 문장을 combine하려면 두 번째 문장의 subject인 "This"가 refer 하는 object를 찾아야 함. Context를 살펴보면 "This"는 첫 번째 문장 전체를 refer하고 있다. 그러므로 두 번째 문장을 back modifier로 만드는 정답은 (A).

Eliminate

(B), (C), (D) "This"가 refer 하는 object는 "thawing", "evidence"가 아님

Q14

Answer : (B)

Category : Vocabulary

Explanation

앞 문장에서는 thawing이 보통 late summer에 일어난다고 했지만, 뒤 문장에서는 2012년 여름에는 평균보다 훨씬 early date인 mid-July에 thawing이 일어났다고 함. 따라서 두 문장의 내용이 반대이므로, opposition을 나타내는 conjunctive adverb를 써야 한다. 정답은 (B)

Eliminate

(A), (C), (D) opposition을 나타내는 conjunctive adverb가 아님

Q15

Answer : (C)

Category : Various Comma Usages

Explanation

"an associate professor of geology at Ohio State" 전체가 "Jason Box"를 꾸며주는 modifying clause임. 이럴 경우 clause의 beginning과 end 둘 다에 comma를 써야 함. 정답은 (C)

Eliminate

(A), (B), (D) comma의 위치가 잘못됨

Q16

Answer : (C)

Category : Colons and Dashes

Explanation

문장에서 "the "dark snow" problem"은 "another factor"가 무엇인지 설명함과 동시에 emphasize되고 있다. 이럴 때 쓰는 punctuation은 colon이나 dash이다. 정답은 (C)

Eliminate

(A), (B) semi-colon을 쓰면 sentence fragment가 생김 / emphasis가 사라짐

(D) "being"은 unnecessary 하며 incoherent clause가 생김

Q17

Answer : (C)

Category : Relative Pronouns

Explanation

Comma 다음에 나오는 dependent clause를 create하기 위해서는 preposition "of"와 relative pronoun "which"가 쓰여야 한다. 정답은 (C)

Eliminate

(A), (B), (C) comma splice가 생김. 두 개의 independent clause를 comma로만 join하는 것은 불가능

Q18

Answer : (A)

Category : Tense Context

Explanation

밑줄 친 verb는 "and then" 다음에 나오므로 앞의 verb들("produced", "drifted")과 같은 tense인 simple past로 쓰여야 한다. 정답은 (A)

Eliminate

(B), (C), (D) "fall"의 simple past tense가 아님.

Q19

Answer : (D)

Category : Number Agreement, Diction

Explanation

밑줄 친 pronoun이 refer하는 object는 plural noun인 "snow and ice"이다. 그러므로 plural pronoun인 "their"가 쓰여야 한다. 정답은 (D)

Eliminate

(A), (B), (C) plural pronoun이 아님

Q20

Answer : (D)

Category : Insert/Delete/Replace

Explanation

Paragraph의 content를 잘 살펴보자. "self-reinforcing cycle"이란 반복적으로 melting이 일어난다는 뜻이다. 반복적인 melting에 대한 내용을 포함한 답은 (D).

Eliminate

(A), (B), (C) melting 이 또 일어난다는 내용 없음

Q21

Answer : (B)

Category : Redundancy, Voice

Explanation

"repeat"이라는 단어가 이미 쓰였으므로, "again"을 또 쓰면 redundant하다. 정답은 (B)

Eliminate

(A), (B) "repeat"와 "again", "damage"와 "harmful effects" : redundant

(D) "possibly"는 나머지 passage의 scientific and objective tone과 맞지 않음

Q22

Answer : (D)

Category : Content Order

Explanation

Paragraph와 sentence 4의 content와 context를 잘 살펴보자. Sentence 4에서 "this crucial information" 라는 내용이 나오므로, paragraph 내에서 crucial information이 mention된 문장 뒤에 넣어야 한다. Sentence 5에서 Box가 "just how much the soot is contributing to the melting of the ice sheet"를 "determine"할 것이라고 한다. 정답은 (D)

Eliminate

(A), (B), (C) paragraph의 logical flow에 방해됨

Q23

Answer : (D)

CategoryCategory : Redundancy

Explanation

"soon"과 "quickly"는 같은 뜻이므로 redundant. 정답은 (D)

Eliminate

(A), (B), (C) "soon", "promptly"는 "quickly"와 redundant

Q24

Answer : (D)
Category : Front Modifier
Explanation

Front modifier인 "Having become frustrated. . ." 가 modify하는 대상은 "I"여야 한다. Modifying clause와 comma 바로 뒤에 "I"가 나오는 정답은 (D).

Eliminate

(A), (B), (C) modifying clause가 "colleagues", "ideas" 를 modify함

Q25

Answer : (B)
Category : Idioms
Explanation

"read A about"이 correct idiomatic expression이다. 정답은 (B)

Eliminate

(A), (C), (D) correct idiomatic expression이 아님

Q26

Answer : (A)
Category : Colons and Dashes
Explanation

"such as" 다음에 list("photocopiers, printers, and fax machines")가 나오므로, colon을 쓸 수 없다. 정답은 (A)

Eliminate

(B), (C) colon은 "such as" 다음에 쓰일 수 없음
(D) main clause와 dependent clause를 "such as" 로 separate할 때는 "such as" 앞에만 comma를 씀

Q27

Answer : (B)
Category : Insert/Delete/Replace
Explanation

바로 앞 문장과 현재 문장의 content를 비교해 보자. 앞 문장에서는 "spaces"에는 "standard office equipment"가 많다는 내용이 나왔고, 현재 문장에서는 "spaces"에 또 어떤 것들이 있는지에 대한 내용이 나왔다. 두 문장을 가장 잘 transition하는 정답은 (B)

Eliminate

(A), (C), (D) 두 문장의 content and relationship을 reflect하지 못함

Q28

Answer : (C)
Category : Insert/Delete/Replace
Explanation

Paragraph 전체와 underlined sentence의 content and context를 잘 살펴보자. Paragraph의 main idea는 coworking space에 equipment와 meeting area 등 여러 가지가 제공된다는 것이다. 하지만 underlined sentence는 이와 관련 없는 cost of launching a new coworking business에 대해 이야기하고 있다. 정답은 (C)

Eliminate

(A), (B) 이 paragraph나 next paragraph의 main topic 과 관련 없음
(D) earlier paragraph에 같은 내용 나온 적 없음

Q29

Answer : (B)
Category : Graph
Explanation

그래프의 내용과 가장 잘 맞는 정답은 (B)이다.

Eliminate

(A) : context 상 맞지 않음. 그 전 문장에서 coworking space가 "melting pots of creativity"라고 했는데, 바로 다음에 coworking spaces가 일을 빨리 끝내는 것을 prevent한다고 말하면 맞지 않음

(C) graph와는 맞지만, 전 문장에서 나오는 "creativity"와 달리 "ideas relating to business"에 대해서 얘기하고 있음

(D) "focus 능력이 12% 증가했다"는 not supported by graph

Q30

Answer : (D)

Category : Subject-Verb Disagreement - Basic, Relative Pronouns

Explanation

문장의 subject인 "people"을 refer하는 relative pronoun은 "who"이다. 또한 "people"은 plural noun이므로 plural verb인 "use"가 쓰여야 한다. 정답은 (D)

Eliminate

(A), (B), (D) "whom"은 문장의 object를 refer하는 relative pronoun/ "uses"는 single verb

Q31

Answer : (C)

Category : Content Order

Explanation

Paragraph와 following sentence의 content and context를 잘 살펴보자. Writer가 새로 add하려는 sentence의 main events는 registration form을 채운 후, work를 시작했다는 것이다. 이 문장은 paragraph 에서 어디에 왜 register하고 work하는 것인지에 대한 내용이 먼저 나온 문장 뒤에 넣어야 logical flow에 맞다. 정답은 (C)

Eliminate

(A), (B), (D) paragraph의 logical flow에 방해됨

Q32

Answer : (A)

Category : Colons and Dashes

Explanation

뒤에 나오는 list ("another website developer, a graphic designer . . .")을 introduce하는 알맞은 punctuation은 colon이다. 정답은 (A)

Eliminate

(B), (C) semi-colon이나 comma를 쓰면 뒤에 나오는 list가 "my coworking colleagues"의 examples라는 것이 unclear해짐

(D) run-on sentence

Q33

Answer : (A)

Category : Voice

Explanation

Passage 전체의 tone을 살펴보자. Personal essay 이므로 casual한 동시에 intelligent한 tone이 쓰였다. Passage 전체의 tone 과 어울리는 정답은 (A)

Eliminate

(B) 너무 colloquial

(C), (D) 너무 formal/ 내용과 맞지 않음 ("proclaim"은 writer가 말하는 colleagues 과의 interaction 에 어울리지 않음)

Q34

Answer : (A)

Category : Vocabulary

Explanation

문장의 context를 잘 살펴보자. 이 문장은 philosophy가 전체적/이론적으로는 어떤 study인지 define하고 있고, 다음 문장은 philosophy를 실생활에 적용하는 방법에 대해 explain한다. 이러한 context에 가장 잘 맞는 conjunctive adverb는 (A)

Eliminate

(B), (C), (D) 이 문장은 앞에 나온 내용의 example 도 아니고 contrast하는 내용도 없음

Q35

Answer : (A)

Category : Wordiness

Explanation

현재 문장은 grammatically correct하며 clear and concise하다. 정답은 (A)

Eliminate

(B), (C), (D) "speaking in a . . . way", "pragmatic-speaking way" 등은 너무 wordy

Q36

Answer : (B)

Category : Incomplete Sentences

Explanation

"Because philosophy . . . how to think"는 뒤의 main clause를 modify하는 adverb clause이다. Adverb clause에는 subject와 verb 둘 다 있어야 한다. 정답은 (B)

Eliminate

(A), (C), (D) adverb clause 에 verb가 빠짐

Q37

Answer : (D)

Category : Insert/Delete/Replace

Explanation

Paragraph 전체와 문장의 content and context를 잘 살펴보자. 지금까지 paragraph는 philosophy의 usefulness에 대해 설명했지만, 뒤에는 1994년도에는 많은 American College들이 philosophy를 중요하게 여기지 않았다는 내용이 나온다. 그러므로 이 두 내용을 가장 잘 transition하는 문장은 (D)

Eliminate

(A), (B), (C) paragraph의 앞부분과 뒷부분의 contrasting relationship 을 잘 reflect하지 않음

Q38

Answer : (C)

Category : Vocabulary

Explanation

이 문장과 앞 문장의 관계를 살펴보자. 앞 문장에서는 1994년에 American College들이 philosophy course를 require하지 않았다는 내용이 나오고, 뒤 문장에서는 이에 덧붙여 1992년과 1996년 사이 400개의 philosophy department가 eliminated되었다는 내용이 나온다. 이러한 addition을 가장 잘 나타낸 conjunctive adverb는 (C)

Eliminate

(A), (B), (D) 두 문장에는 cause-and-effect / contrast 내용 없음

Q39

Answer : (A)

Category : Wordiness

Explanation

두 문장을 가장 clear and concise하게 combine하는 답은 (A)이다.

Eliminate

(B), (C), (D) 너무 wordy

Q40

Answer : (B)

Category : Subject-Verb Disagreement, Incomplete Sentence

Explanation

이 문장의 subject는 plural noun인 "students" 이므로 plural verb인 "have scored"가 쓰여야 한다.

Eliminate

(A), (C) single verb임

(D) 문장에 verb가 없어져 incomplete sentence가 됨

Q41

Answer : (B)
Category : Back Modifier, Apostrophes
Explanation
　이 문장의 verb는 "have" 이다. "intention"을 "have"할 수 있는 것은 "majoring"이 아닌 "students"이므로, "majoring"을 back modifier 로 바꾸기 위해 "students'"의 apostrophe를 제거 해야 한다. 정답은 (B)
Eliminate
　(A), (D) subject가 "majoring", "majors"가 됨
　(C) run-on sentence

Q42

Answer : (C)
Category : Insert/Delete/Replace
Explanation
　Paragraph와 주어진 문장의 content and context 를 잘 살펴보자. 주어진 문장에서 "for example"이 라는 phrase와 함께 Plato가 dialogue의 form을 썼다는 내용이 나왔으므로, 그 앞에 dialogue form 에 대한 내용이 나왔어야 add하는 것이 적절하다. 하지만 paragraph 에서는 지금까지 philosoph 의 usefulness에 대한 내용만 나왔고 form of dialogues에 대한 내용은 없었다. 정답은 (C)
Eliminate
　(A), (B) paragraph의 main idea나 counterarguement와 관련 없음
　(D) employability of philosophy majors와 관 련 없음

Q43

Answer : (D)
Category : Incomplete Sentences
Explanation
　이 문장의 subject는 "That these skills . . . across professions"라는 phrase 전체이고, verb는 "makes"이다. 정답은 (D)
Eliminate
　(A), (B), (C) 문장에 verb가 없어짐/ subject와 verb 사이에 "and" 쓰일 수 없음

Q44

Answer : (D)
Category : Pronoun Shift
Explanation
　이 pronoun이 refer하는 object는 "today's students" 이다. 이에 맞는 posessive pronoun은 "their"이다. 정답은 (D)
Eliminate
　(A), (B), (C) "today's students"의 possessive pronoun으로 적절치 않음

Section 3. Math Test
(No Calculator)

Q1
Answer : (D)
Category : Equations
Explanation

$k=3$
$\frac{x-1}{3}=k \rightarrow \frac{x-1}{3}=3$
$x-1=9 \rightarrow x=10$
$\therefore$ D

Q2
Answer : (A)
Category : Numbers
Explanation

Complex Number를 더할 때는 real part와 imaginary part를 따로 더한다.
$(7+3i)+(-8+9i)$
$\rightarrow (7+(-8))=-1$
$\rightarrow (3i+9i)=12i$
$(-1+12i)$
$\therefore$ A

Q3
Answer : (C)
Category : Rate
Explanation

보낸 message의 수
=message 보낸 시간 × message 보내는 rate
Armand $\rightarrow 5 \times m \frac{\text{texts}}{\text{hour}}$
Tyrone $\rightarrow 4 \times p \frac{\text{texts}}{\text{hour}}$
둘의 합은 $5m+4p$
$\therefore$ C

Q4
Answer : (B)
Category : Equations
Explanation

$P=108-23d$에서 d는 days worked, P는 number of phones left to fix이므로 d가 0일 경우 Kathy가 고칠 phone은 108이다. Kathy가 일을 하지 않은 0일째, 고칠 phone은 108이라는 것을 볼 때, 108은 주가 시작할 때 Kathy가 받는 일주일 동안 고칠 phone의 수이다.
$\therefore$ B

Q5
Answer : (C)
Category : Equations
Explanation

같은 term끼리 combine하면
$(x^2y-3y^2+5xy^2)-(-x^2y+3xy^2-3y^2)$
$=2x^2y+0+2xy^2 \rightarrow 2x^2y+2xy^2$
$\therefore$ C

Q6
Answer : (A)
Category : Equations
Explanation

$h=3a+28.6$일 때, a가 나이이고, 1만큼 increase하면 $h=3(a+1)+28.6 \rightarrow h=(3a+28.6)+3$인 것을 볼 때, 한 살이 늘 때 3 inch 가 클 것이라고 예상할 수 있다.
$\therefore$ A

Q7

Answer : (B)

Category : Equations

Explanation

$$m = \frac{\left(\frac{r}{1,200}\right)\left(1+\frac{r}{1,200}\right)^N}{\left(1-\frac{r}{1,200}\right)^N - 1} P$$

$$m \frac{\left(1+\frac{r}{1,200}\right)^N - 1}{\left(\frac{r}{1,200}\right)\left(1-\frac{r}{1,200}\right)^N} = P$$

∴ B

Q8

Answer : (C)

Category : Ratio

Explanation

$\frac{a}{b} = 2 \rightarrow \frac{b}{a} = \frac{1}{2} \rightarrow \frac{4b}{a} = 2$

∴ C

Q9

Answer : (B)

Category : Equations

Explanation

$3x + 4y = -23$ ······ ①

$-x + 2y = -19$ ······ ②

① $- 2 \times$ ② $\rightarrow 5x = 15$

$x = 3, y = -8$

∴ B

Q10

Answer : (A)

Category : Functions

Explanation

$g(x)$는 even function이므로, $g(4) = g(-4)$.

$g(4) = 8 = g(-4)$

∴ A

Q11

Answer : (D)

Category : Equations

Explanation

b(price per pound of beef)와 c(price per pound of chicken)가 같을 때를 표현하면,

$b = c = 2.35 + 0.25x = 1.75 + 0.40x \rightarrow x = 4$

그러므로 $b = 3.35$

∴ D

Q12

Answer : (D)

Category : Coordinate Geometry

Explanation

모든 origin을 pass하는 line의 equation은 $y = mx$ 이다. m은 slope이므로, 이 line 의 equation은 $y = \frac{1}{7}x$이다.

∴ D

Q13

Answer : (B)

Category : Equations

Explanation

$$\frac{1}{\frac{1}{(x+2)} + \frac{1}{(x+3)}} \rightarrow \frac{1}{\frac{(x+3)+(x+2)}{(x+2)(x+3)}}$$

$$\rightarrow \frac{(x+2)(x+3)}{(x+3)+(x+2)}$$

∴ B

Q14

Answer : (A)

Category : Powers and Roots

Explanation

$\frac{8^x}{2^y} = \frac{2^{3x}}{2^y} \rightarrow 2^{3x-y} \rightarrow 2^{12}$

∴ A

Q15
Answer : (D)
Category : Equations
Explanation

$(ax+2)(bx+7)=15x^2+cx+14$
$abx^2+7ax+2bx+14=15x^2+cx+14$
$ab=15 \to a=8-b \to a^2-8a+15=0$
$(a-3)(a-5)=0$이므로, a와 b는
$a=3, b=5$일 수도, $a=5, b=3$ 일 수도 있다.
첫 번째일 경우, $15x^2+31x+14$이므로, $c=31$.
두 번째일 경우, $15x^2+41x+14$이므로, $c=41$.
∴ D

Q16
Answer : 2
Category : Equations
Explanation

$t^2-4=0 \to t^2=4 \to t=2$ 또는 $t=-2$
$t>0$ 이므로 $t=2$.
∴ 2

Q17
Answer : 1,600
Category : Triangles
Explanation

∠AEB=∠CDB이고, ∠ABE와 ∠CBD가 vertical angles이므로, ∠ABE=∠CBD. 삼각형 EAB는 삼각형 DCB와 두 pair 의 congruent corresponding angles를 가지고 있으므로, 둘은 similar하다. 그러므로 $\dfrac{\overline{CD}}{x}=\dfrac{\overline{BD}}{\overline{EB}} \to$
$\dfrac{800}{x}=\dfrac{700}{1,400} \to x=1,600$.
∴ 1,600

Q18
Answer : 7
Category : Equations
Explanation

$x+y=-9$ ······ ①
$x+2y=-25$ ······ ②
① − ② $\to y=-16 \to x=7$
∴ 7

Q19
Answer : $\dfrac{4}{5}$ or 6.25
Category : Trigonometry
Explanation

Sine과 cosine의 complementary angle relationship에 의하면, $\sin x = \cos(90-x)$ 이므로, $\cos(90-x)=\dfrac{4}{5}$.
∴ $\dfrac{4}{5}$ or 6.25

Q20
Answer : 100
Category : Powers and Roots
Explanation

$2a=\sqrt{2x}, \ a=5\sqrt{2} \to 10\sqrt{2}=\sqrt{2x} \to 200=2x$
$x=100$.
∴ 100

Section 4. Math Test
(Calculator)

Q1
Answer : (B)
Category : Graphs and Data Analysis
Explanation
그래프는 John의 heart rate를 표기한다. Strictly increasing할 때는 slope가 positive이고, strictly decreasing할 때는 slope가 negative이므로, 40분에서 60분의 heart rate가 오로지 그 slope들을 보여준다.
∴ B

Q2
Answer : (C)
Category : Equations
Explanation
y가 24이고 x가 6일 때, k는 4이다. k는 constant이므로, $y=4x$이고, x가 5라면 y는 20이다.
∴ C

Q3
Answer : (D)
Category : Polygons
Explanation

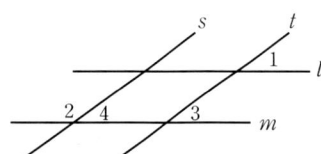

∠3과 ∠1은 corresponding angles이므로, ∠3=∠1이다. ∠3과 ∠4도 corresponding angles이므로, ∠3=∠4이고, ∠1=∠3=∠4이다. ∠2와 ∠4는 supplementary이므로, 둘의 합이 180°이어야 한다.
∠2=$(180-35)°=145°$
∴ D

Q4
Answer : (C)
Category : Equations
Explanation
"$16+4x$ is 10 more than 14"는 수식으로 $16+4x=10+14$로 쓰여질 수 있다.
$4x=8 \rightarrow 8x=16$.
∴ C

Q5
Answer : (D)
Category : Graphs and Data Analysis
Explanation
A strong negative association을 보여주는 그래프는 line of best fit이 negative slope를 보여줘야 한다.
∴ D

Q6
Answer : (D)
Category : Ratio
Explanation
$$\frac{2 \text{ decagrams}}{1} \times \frac{10 \text{ grams}}{1 \text{ decagram}}$$
$$\times \frac{1{,}000 \text{ milligrams}}{1 \text{ gram}}$$
$$=20{,}000 \text{ miligrams}$$
∴ D

Q7

Answer : (C)

Category : Graphs and Data Analysis

Explanation

Total number of installation이 27,500이고, 제일 큰 값인 9와 proportion이 맞으려면, vertical axis는 thousands로 수를 세어야 한다.

∴ C

Q8

Answer : (D)

Category : Equations, Absolute Value

Explanation

$|n-1|+1=0 \rightarrow |n-1|=-1$

하지만 $|n-1|$는 오로지 positive value만 output 하므로, $|n-1|$는 -1이 될 수 없다.

∴ D

Q9

Answer : (A)

Category : Equations

Explanation

$a=1{,}052+1.08t$를 t에 대해 정리하면

$t=\dfrac{a-1{,}052}{1.08}$이다.

∴ A

Q10

Answer : (B)

Category : Equations

Explanation

$a=1{,}052+1.08t \rightarrow 1{,}000=1{,}052+1.08t$

$t \approx -48.15$이므로, 제일 가까운 값이 답이다.

∴ B

Q11

Answer : (A)

Category : Equations

Explanation

$3x-5 \geq 4x-3 \rightarrow -2 \geq x$

x가 답이 되려면, -2보다 작거나 같은 값이어야 한다. 보기 중에서 -2보다 작은 값은 -1뿐이다.

∴ A

Q12

Answer : (C)

Category : Graphs and Data Analysis

Explanation

Average number of seeds per apple

$=\dfrac{\text{Number of seeds}}{\text{Total number of apples}}$

씨의 수는 graph를 통해 구할 수 있다. $\dfrac{73}{12}=6.08$

∴ C

Q13

Answer : (C)

Category : Graphs and Data Analysis

Explanation

"All the survey respondents"$=310$

"Approximately 19% of all the survey respondents" 는 $19 \times 310=58.90$이며, 제일 가까운 값이 답이다.

∴ C

Q14

Answer : (C)

Category : Graphs and Data Analysis

Explanation

Table에서 24가 빠진다면, Range는 $16-8=8$이며, $24-8=16$에서 8이 바뀌었으므로 median이나 mean이 바뀌는 값보다 더 많이 바뀌게 된다.

∴ C

Q15

Answer : (A)

Category : Graphs and Data Analysis

Explanation

그래프를 보고, 시간이 0 hour 일 때, total cost 는 5 dollars인 것을 볼 수 있다. Boat를 쓰지 않았을 때 5 dollars를 내야 하는 것으로 볼 때, 5 dollars는 boat를 빌릴 때 내야 하는 값인 것을 알 수 있다.

∴ A

Q16

Answer : (C)

Category : Graphs and Data Analysis

Explanation

line의 slope $= \dfrac{y_2 - y_1}{x_2 - x_1} = 3$

$y = mx + b$에 적용하면 $b = y-\text{intercept} = 5$

∴ C

Q17

Answer : (B)

Category : Graphs and Data Analysis

Explanation

$f(x)$의 minimum값은 $f(x)$의 $y-$value가 제일 낮은 point다.

∴ B

Q18

Answer : (A)

Category : Equations

Explanation

$(0, 0)$이 system of inequalities의 solution이다.

$(0, 0)$이 inequalities들에 적용됐을 때,

$y < -x + a \ \to 0 < a$

$y > x + b \ \to 0 > b$이고,

$0 < a, 0 > b$인 것을 보았을 때, a는 positive number, b는 negative number이라는 것을 알 수 있다.

∴ A

Q19

Answer : (B)

Category : Equations

Explanation

x가 salad의 갯수, y가 drink의 개수라고 가정하면,

$6.50x + 2.00y = 836.50$

$x + y = 209 \to x = 93$

∴ B

Q20

Answer : (D)

Category : Percentage, Equations

Explanation

x를 computer의 원래 가격으로 가정하면, sale price는 $0.8x$, 그리고 tax는 $0.08(0.8x)$이다. Total amount Alma paid

$p = 0.08(0.8x) + 0.8x = 1.08(0.8x)$

∴ D

Q21

Answer : (C)

Category : Probability, Graphs and Data Analysis

Explanation

"At least 1 dream"을 기억한 사람들의 수는 $39 + 125 = 164$이다. Group Y에서 적어도 1개의 꿈을 기억한 사람의 수는 $11 + 68 = 79$ 이다. "the probability that the person who recalled at least 1 dream from Group Y"는 $\dfrac{79}{164}$이다.

∴ C

Q22

Answer : (B)

Category : Graphs and Data Analysis, Functions

Explanation

"The average rate of change in the annual budget for agriculture/natural resources in Kansas from 2008 to 2010"

$$= \frac{\text{total change (in thousands of dollars)}}{\text{number of years}}$$

$$\frac{488,106 - 358,708}{2} \times 1000\ (\$) \cong 65,000,000$$

∴ B

Q23

Answer : (B)

Category : Ratio, Graphs and Data Analysis

Explanation

"Human resources program's ratio of its 2007 budget to its 2010 budget"은 $\frac{4,051,050}{5,921,379}$ 로, $\frac{4}{6}$ 정도로, $\frac{2}{3}$ 로 estimate할 수 있다. 보기 중에서 이와 제일 근접한 답은 education의 2007 budget과 2010 budget의 ratio로 $\frac{2}{3}$ 이다.

∴ B

Q24

Answer : (A)

Category : Circle Equation

Explanation

Equation of a circle은 $(x-h)^2 + (y-k)^2 = r^2$이다. (h, k)는 circle 의 center coordinates이고, r은 circle의 radius이다. Center coordinates은 주어졌고, r은 center에서 endpoint까지이므로, distance formula로 구할 수 있다.

$r^2 = \left(\frac{4}{3} - 0\right)^2 + (5-4)^2 = \frac{25}{9}$이므로,

∴ A

Q25

Answer : (D)

Category : Functions

Explanation

공은 h가 0일 때 땅에 떨어질 것이다.

$0 = -4.9t^2 + 25t$

$t = 0$와 $t = \frac{25}{4.9} \approx 5.1$이다.

$t = 0$는 공이 땅에서 던져졌을 때이므로

∴ D

Q26

Answer : (B)

Category : Percentage

Explanation

Type B trees가 produce하는 pears 개수를 "x"라고 하면 $x + 0.20x = 1.20x$

$1.20x$가 type A tree가 생산하는 수이므로

$1.20x = 144$

∴ B

Q27

Answer : (C)

Category : Fractions, Graphs and Data Analysis

Explanation

학생들이 찾은 지렁이의 수를 average하면, 147.1이 된다. 하지만, 한 학생이 맡은 구역의 area는 total area의 $\frac{1}{100}$ 밖에 되지 않는다. 한 학생이 찾은 지렁이의 average를 100으로 곱해야 "a reasonable approximation of the earthworms to a depth of 5 centimeters beneath the ground's surface in the entire field"를 찾을 수 있다.

∴ C

Q28

Answer : (C)
Category : Functions
Explanation

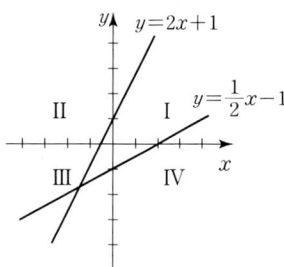

그래프를 그려보면, Quadrant I, II, 그리고 III까지 닿으니까, 두 그래프의 solution은 윗부분이라는 것을 알 수 있다.
∴ C

Q29

Answer : (D)
Category : Functions
Explanation

$p(x)$가 polynomial이고 $p(3)=-2$이므로
$p(x)=(x-3)Q(x)-2$
$x-3$으로 $p(x)$를 나누면 remainder $=-2$
∴ D

Q30

Answer : (D)
Category : Functions
Explanation

$y=x^2-2x-15$
$\quad=(x-1)^2-1-15$
$\quad=(x-1)^2-16$
∴ D

Q31

Answer : any number between 4 and 6, inclusive
Category : Rate
Explanation

Wyatt이 제일 느려도 $\frac{72}{12}=6$ hours 에 72 dozen ears of corn을 husk할 수 있고, 제일 빠를 때에는 $\frac{72}{18}=4$ hours 에 72 dozen ears of corn을 husk 할 수 있으므로, 4시간에서 6시간 사이 안에는 72 dozen ears of corn을 husk할 수 있다.
∴ any number between 4 and 6, inclusive

Q32

Answer : 107
Category : Equations
Explanation

박스들의 개수가 트럭에 주는 무게는 $14x$로 구할 수 있다. 빈 트럭과 운전수의 합한 무게는 4,500 pound이므로 "the maximum possible value for x that will keep the combined weight of the truck, driver, and boxes below the bridge's posted weight limit"은 $6,000 > 14x+4,500$으로 찾을 수 있다.
∴ 107

Q33

Answer : $\frac{5}{8}$ or 0.625
Category : Fractions
Explanation

$\frac{\text{number of players sold in 2008}}{\text{number of players sold in 2011}}=\frac{100}{160}$

∴ $\frac{5}{8}$ or 0.625

Q34

Answer : 96

Category : Ratio

Explanation

$\dfrac{2 \text{ \sout{days}}}{1 \text{ week}} \times \dfrac{24 \text{ \sout{hours}}}{1 \text{ \sout{day}}} \times \dfrac{60 \text{ minutes}}{1 \text{ \sout{hour}}}$
$= 2,880$

한 time slot이 30 minutes이므로,

$\dfrac{2,880 \text{ minutes}}{30 \text{ minutes}}$ 로 "total number of 30-minute time slots the station can sell for Tuesday and Wednesday"를 구할 수 있다.

∴ 96

Q35

Answer : 6

Category : Solids

Explanation

Cylinder의 volume은 $\pi r^2 h$로 구할 수 있다.

Volume
$= \pi r^2 h = 8\pi r^2 = 72\pi$
→ $r^2 = 9$
　$r = 3$
　$2r = 6$

∴ 6

Q36

Answer : 3

Category : Functions

Explanation

Function h는 denominator가 0일 때 undefined 이다.

$(x-5)^2 + 4(x-5) + 4 = ((x-5)+2)^2$
$\hspace{4.5cm} = (x-3)^2$

∴ 3

Q37

Answer : 1.02

Category : Powers and Roots, Equations

Explanation

2 percent interest compounded annually이므로, 매해 2퍼센트의 increase를 표현하면 1.02 이다.

∴ 1.02

Q38

Answer : 6.11

Category : Powers and Roots, Equations

Explanation

Jessica의 expression을 쓰면, Jessica의 account는 10년 후에 $\$100(1.02)^{10} = \$121.899$ 인 것을 알 수 있다. Tyshaun의 account value는 $\$100(1.025)^{10}$ 로 구할 수 있으므로, 두 값의 difference를 찾으면 된다.

∴ 6.11

Part 2

Practice Test #2

Part II Practice Test #2

Section 1. Reading Test

Passage I. "The Professor"

Passage Summary

Lines

- **1-6:** No one likes to admit that they made a mistake and need to be doing something else as a profession.
- **7-27:** My job of translating business letter was boring, but that wasn't the only problem. If it was I could have handled it happily.
- **28-33:** It was boring AND my boss and I hated each other.
- **34-43:** He hated everything about me, especially because he was jealous of me and feared me as a rival.
- **44-56:** If I had been weak or worse than him in any way, he probably would have been ok, but I was just too smart and it drove him crazy. He kept waiting for me to make a mistake of any kind.
- **57-74:** One day after I got paid, I was thinking about how much my boss hated paying me, and I started to think about how I could get out of my terrible situation. I went from feeling unhappy but dealing with it, to actively looking how to improve my situation.

Main Idea

The narrator hates his job because it is boring, but mostly because his boss doesn't like him.

Tone

Dramatic, wordy, slightly ironic

Vocabulary

Line 5	baffle	v.	완전히 당황하게 만들다; 도저히 이해할 수 없다
Line 5	submit to	v.	항복(굴복)하다, (굴복하여) ~하기로 하다
Line 7	irksome	a.	짜증 나는, 귀찮은
Line 9	tedious	a.	지루한, 싫증 나는
Line 10	nuisance	n.	성가신(귀찮은) 사람(것, 일), 골칫거리
Line 14	tradesman	n.	방문 판매원, 배달원
Line 15	rust	n.	녹
Line 15	cramp	n.	(근육에 생기는) 경련[쥐]
Line 15	faculty	n.	(사람이 타고 나는 신체적, 정신적) 능력[기능]
Line 17	pent	v.	'pen'의 과거분사 / (동물, 사람을 우리 등에) 가두다
Line 19	monotony	n.	단조로움
Line 20	tumult	n.	소란, 소동
Line 20	panting	a.	헐떡거리는, 가슴이 두근거리는
Line 23	lodging	n.	임시 숙소, 하숙
Line 25	cherished–in–secret	a.	비밀리에 간직된
Line 27	severe	v.	극심한, 심각한
Line 28	antipathy	n.	(강한) 반감
Line 33	slimy	a.	(더럽고) 끈적끈적한, 점액질의
Line 37	trifling	a.	하찮은, 사소한
Line 39	evince	v.	(감정, 특질을) 분명히 밝히다[피력하다]
Line 40	irritate	v.	짜증나게 하다, 거슬리다
Line 42	poignant	n.	가슴 아픈[저미는]
Line 42	relish	n.	(큰) 즐거움, 기쁨
Line 44	inferior	a.	(~보다) 못한[질 낮은, 열등한]
Line 47	padlock	n.	맹꽁이자물쇠
Line 48	sharer	n.	함께 하는 사람, 공유자
Line 49	mortifying	a.	분한, 원통한; 고행의
Line 51	prowl	v.	(특히 먹이를 찾아 살금살금) 돌아다니다
Line 52	pry	v.	엿보다, 파고들다, 꼬치꼬치 캐다
Line 52	malignity	n.	악의, 앙심, 원한
Line 53	lynx–eyes	n.	날카로운 눈
Line 53	sentinel	n.	보초병, 감시병
Line 54	malice	n.	악의, 적의
Line 54	tact	n.	요령, 눈치, 재치
Line 56	slumber	n.	잠, 수면
Line 60	grudge	v.	(무엇을 하거나 주는 것을) 억울해 하다, 아까워하다
Line 61	pittance	n.	(먹고 살기에 턱없이 부족한) 아주 적은[얼마 안 되는] 돈

Line 63	inexorable	a.	멈출[변경할] 수 없는, 거침 없는
Line 66	monotonous	a.	(지루할 정도로) 단조로운, 변함 없는
Line 74	gleam	n.	어슴푸레한[흐릿한] 빛

Questions

Q1 THING: Main Idea

Answer Key : (A)

Line 7에서 자기 일이 "irksome"하다고 admit한 다음, 왜 그런지 여러 가지 이유를 말하고 있다. Line 9에서는 일이 "dry and tedious"하다고 describe하고, line 28–31에서 "the antipathy which had sprung up between myself and my employer striking deeper … daily"라고 한다.

Second best answer: (B)

Employer는 narrator가 자기보다 잘 하는 걸 볼 때 싫어한다는 내용은 mentioned. 하지만 서로 compete하는 것이 passage의 focus는 아님

Eliminate

(B) compete하는 것이 passage의 focus가 아님
(C), (D) not mentioned

Q2 THING: Main Idea, Quote

Answer Key : (D)

첫 문장에서는 사람들은 자기 직업을 잘못 골랐다고 admit하는 것을 싫어하고 힘들어도 대부분 계속 한다는 내용이다. 지금 narrator가 자기 직업을 싫어하면서도 employer와 나쁜 사이만 아니면 계속 했을 것이라는 idea를 support해 준다.

Eliminate

A), (D) controversy, evidence of malicious conduct는 not mentioned
(C) Edward Crimsworth에 focus하고 있지 않음

Q3 THING: Main Idea, List

Answer Key : (C)

General: 사람들이 직업을 선택하고 나서 후회할 때 어떻게 하는지 → specific: 자기가 일을 왜 싫어하는지.

Second best answer: (D)

unhappy하게 만드는 factor들을 설명해 주기는 하지만, alternative들을 구체적으로 얘기하지 않음

Eliminate

(A), (B), (D) narrator's self-doubt, expectations of life, alternatives가 paragraph의 focus는 아님

Q4 THING: Tone

Answer Key : (A)

Lines 27–33에서 narrator가 자신의 employer와의 안 좋은 관계에 대해서 얘기한다. 그런 employer와 함께 일하는 것을 "shade"와 "humid darkness"에서 살고 있는 것에 compare한다. 이런 단어들은 narrator가 자기 직업과 employer에 대해 느끼는 unhappiness를 보여준다.

Eliminate

(B), (C), (D) narrator의 sinister thoughts, fear of confinement, longing for rest와 관련없음

Q5 THING: Main Idea, List

Answer Key : (D)

Line 43에서 Crimsworth는 narrator가 "successful trader"가 될까봐 걱정한다고 하고, lines 44–48에서 narrator가 자신은 갖지 못한 "mental wealth"를 narrator가 숨겨두고 있는 것을 싫어한다는 점을 얘기한다. 즉 Crimsworth는 narrator's superiority에 jealousy를 느끼고 있다.

Eliminate

(A), (C) line 51에서 narrator가 자신은 "Caution, Tact, Observation"을 가지고 있다고 하므로, high spirits나 rash actions과 맞지 않음

(B) humble background는 not mentioned

Q6 THING: Point of View, Contrasting Pair

Answer Key : (B)

Lines 61–62에서 narrator가 더이상 Crimsworth를 "brother"로 생각하지 않는다고 한다. 여기서 "brother"는 ally라는 뜻도 가지고 있다. 즉 예전에는 Crimsworth를 ally라고 생각한 적이 있다는 것이다.

Eliminate:

(A), (C) (D) harmless rival, perceptive judge, demanding mentor는 not mentioned

Q7 THING: Line Evidence

Answer Key : (D)

6번 문제 답의 keyword인 "sympathetic ally"가 나오는 lines를 찾아보자. "Lines 61–62에서 narrator가 "had long ceased to regard Mr. Crimsworth as my brother"라고 한다. 이것은 keyword의 synonym으로 볼 수 있다.

Eliminate:

(A), (B), (C) keyword나 keyword synonym이 나오지 않음

Q8 THING: Contrasting Pair

Answer Key : (D)

Lines 48–53에서 narrator는 "Caution, Tact, Observation"을 열심히 지키면서 Crimsworth를 "lynx-like eyes"로 watch했다고 한다. Lines 53–56에서는 Crimsworth가 narrator를 watch하면서 narrator가 실수를 하면 "steal snake-like"할 준비를 하고 있다는 것을 말한다. 즉 Crimsworth는 narrator가 실수하면 shame하고 싶어한다. Lynx vs. snake는 narrator와 Crimsworth의 관계를 보여준다.

Eliminate

(A), (B) hypothetical courses of action, resolution은 not mentioned

(C) lines 48–56에서 Crimsworth가 narrator를 blame하려고 노력하는 것을 보여주지만, 둘 사이에 alternation이 생길 것을 보여주지 않음

Q9 THING: Contrasting Pair, Problem

Answer Key : (D)

Lines 48–49에서 narrator는 자신의 방에 있는 fireplace에 fire의 "cheering red gleam"이 없다는 것을 notice한다. "cheering"한 것이 없다는 것은 narrator가 자신의 방을 dreary하게 여긴다는 것을 나타낸다.

Eliminate

(A), (D) not mentioned

(C) lines 69–74에서 자기 방에 불이 있을까 wonder하고 있으므로 자기가 사는 곳에 대해서 predict할 수 없다는 것을 알 수 있음

Q10 THING: Line Evidence

Answer Key : (D)

9번 문제의 keywords인 "living quarters", "dreary"가 subject로 나오는 lines를 찾아보자. Lines 68–74에서 narrator는 "my lodgings"에 대해 "no cheering gleam" 이라고 한다. 이것은 keywords의 synonym으로 볼 수 있다.

Eliminate

(A), (C) 자기 방에 대한 narrator의 opinion not mentioned

(B) lines 21–23는 방을 "small"하다고만 describe함

Passage II. "Can Economics Be Ethical?"

Passage Summary

Lines

1-10: People have been asking more about economic morality lately. Some say markets are naturally ethical, while others say corporations need to take responsibility. In order to answer this question, though, we need to define the topic.

11-30: First, what exactly is ethical? Adam Smith said that sometimes not being empathic in the short run makes things better for everyone in the long run. People and organizations are rarely empathetic, which is selfish of them.

31-44: Aristotle said ethics was about character, such as making the right decisions at the right time based on values like courage and honesty. However, these values are really hard to define.

45-56: A third perspective is that focusing on our individual actions and choices rather than character or consequences is easier to follow. However, this approach can be too restrictive since it can prevent us from taking necessary actions because it is "bad" in the moment.

57-66: It may seem like these three methods don't work well together, but it is still possible to be ethical since they often agree with one another.

67-77: Rules don't work because people are irrational.

78-end: Some studies have been working on how we make ethical considerations and decisions, which might solve this problem altogether.

Main Idea

There are three different ways to think about ethics in economics. Studying psychology might help define ethics for economists.

Tone

Informative, contemplative

Vocabulary

Line 7	embrace	v.	(껴)안다, 포옹하다
Line 9	sneer	v.	비웃다, 조롱하다
Line 19	counter-productive	a.	의도와 반대되는 결과를 초래하는; 비생산적인

Line 20	better off	형편이 더 나은
Line 39	corporate raider	기업 매수자
Line 41	extreme	n. 극단
Line 45	root	v. (무엇을 찾기 위해) 파헤치다, 뒤지다
Line 51	commandment	n. (특히 성경의) 계명
Line 52	devalue	v. 가치를 낮춰 보다, 평가 절하하다
Line 57	dilemma	n. 딜레마
Line 58	clash	n. (두 집단 간의 짧은 물리적) 충돌; 차이
Line 59	inevitable	a. 불가피한, 필연적인
Line 63	virtuous	a. 도덕적인, 고결한
Line 64	flawed	a. 결함[결점, 흠]이 있는
Line 64	common ground	공통되는 기반, 공통점
Line 67	queasy	a. 욕지기나는, 메스꺼운
Line 69	phony	a. 가짜의, 허위의; 겉치레의
Line 71	parody	n. 패러디 (다른 것을 풍자적으로 모방한 글, 음악, 연극 등)
Line 75	herd	n. (함께 살고 함께 먹이를 먹는 동종 짐승의) 떼
Line 78	quirk	n. (사람의 성격에서) 별난 점; 기벽
Line 80	neuroscientist	n. 신경과학자
Line 84	disgust	n. 혐오감, 역겨움, 넌더리
Line 85	injustice	n. 불평등; 부당함, 부당성
Line 88	emerge	v. (어둠 속이나 숨어있던 곳에서) 나오다[모습을 드러내다]

Questions

Q11 THING: Main Idea

Answer Key : (D)

Lines 11–12에서 "different views on where ethics should apply when someone makes an economic decision"을 주제로 설명하고 있다. 이 passage에서 유명한 경제학자들이 ethics와 economics 사이의 relationships에 대해서 어떻게 생각했는지 설명한다.

Eliminate

(A), (B), (C) too specific

Q12 THING: Point of View

Answer Key : (D)

Lines 4–5에서 사람들은 free market 자체가 ethical하다고 생각하기 때문에 ethics를 따로 또 criticize하는 것은 unnecessary하다고 생각한다고 주장한다. 벌써 personal decision으로 돌아가는 market은 ethical하다고 생각한다.

Eliminate

(A), (B) free markets에서 ethics를 criticize하고 있지 않음

(C) free markets가 devalued currency에 depend한다는 내용 not mentioned

Q13 THING: Line Evidence

Answer Key : (A)

12번 문제의 keywords인 "objections", "criticizing the ethics of free markets"가 나오는 lines를 찾아보자. Lines 4–5에서 사람들은 free market들은 "personal choice"를 allow하므로 "already ethical"이라고 생각한다고 말한다.

Eliminate

(B), (C), (D) keywords가 나오지 않음

Q14 THING: Vocabulary

Answer Key : (B)

Lines 6–7에서 사람들은 "accepted the ethical critique and embraced corporate social responsibility"라고 함 → context 상 "embrace"는 specific 행동을 하면서 corporate social responsibility를 accept한다는 의미이다.

Eliminate

(A), (C), (D) wrong meaning in context

Q15 THING: Main Idea

Answer Key : (C)

Fifth paragraph는 Aristotle이나 Adam Smith의 ethics 대신 세 번째 정의를 알려준다. Lines 45–48에 "instead of rooting ethics in character or the consequences of actions, we can focus on our actions themselves ... some things are right, some wrong"이라고 한다.

Eliminate

(A) fifth paragraph에서 counterargument는 not mentioned

(B), (D) "character"가 잠깐 나오지만 ethics와의 관계는 fourth paragraph의 focus

Q16 THING: Vocabulary

Answer Key : (A)

Lines 57–59에서 "three versions pull in different directions"할 때 conflict가 inevitable하지는 않다고 함 → context 상 "clash"는 "pull in different directions", 즉 conflict를 의미한다.

Eliminate

(B), (C), (D) wrong meaning in context

Q17 THING: Main Idea, List

Answer Key : (C)

Lines 59–64에서 fair trade coffee에 대해서 얘기하면서 Adam Smith, Aristotle, 그리고 세 번째 approach 모두 적용될 수 있다고 한다. 모두 다 "common ground"(line 64)가 있어서 같이 적용되어도 서로 contradict하지 않는다.

Eliminate

(A) "different views on ethics"를 얘기하지만 어떻게 같이 적용될 수 있는지는 얘기하지 않음

(B) 세 번째 ethical economics만 얘기함

(D) 사람들은 economics에 대해서 행동할 때 "herd"같다고 함

Q18 THING: Main Idea

Answer Key : (C)

Lines 83–88에서 psychology를 통해서 사람들의 reactions를 더 잘 이해하고 ethics를 define할 수 있다고 한다.

Eliminate

(A), (B) 마지막 paragraph의 main idea가 아닌, discuss되었던 topics

(D) economists가 responsible하다는 내용 not mentioned

Q19 THING: Graph

Answer Key : (A)

Graph를 보면, 2000~2008 사이에 Tanzania에서의 fair trade coffee는 $1.30 per pound profit을 얻고, regular coffee는 20–60 cents per pound였다.

Eliminate

(B), (C), (D) not supported by graph

Q20 THING: Graph

Answer Key : (B)

Graph에서 2002–2004 사이에 fair trade coffee와 regular coffee의 profit 차이는 $1 정도 된다고 보여준다. Fair trade coffee의 가격은 계속 stable했지만, regular coffee 가격이 갑자기 떨어지면서 이 기간의 profit 차이가 가장 크다.

Eliminate

(A), (C), (D) fair trade와 regular coffee의 greatest difference between per–pound profits를 보여주지 않음

Q21 THING: Graph

Answer Key : (C)

Lines 59–61에서 fair trade coffee를 "coffee that is sold with a certification that indicates the farmers and workers who produced it were paid a fair wage"로 define한다. 즉 fair trade coffee는 ethically responsible하면서도 profitable하다고 주장한다. Graph에서 fair trade coffee가 regular coffee보다 훨씬 더 profitable한 것을 보여주면서 지문을 support하고 있다.

Eliminate

(A) graph에서 empathy로 사는 것도 profitable할 수 있다고 보여줌

(B), (D) not supported by graph

Passage III. "The Web Shatters Focus" / "Mind Over Mass Media"

Passage 1

Passage Summary

Lines

1-13: Some cognitive skills are strengthened by using computers and the Internet.

14-22: Web browsing also strengthens some areas of the brain.

23-38: However, according to a Science article, although using the Internet does strengthen visual–spatial skills, it also weakens our capacity for "deep processing."

39-50: Our brain will change during the time we are on the Internet, so that even when we are offline we will keep using the same areas of the brain.

Main Idea

The Internet and computers have made us better at skills that are useful on the Internet, like visual/spatial literacy and problem solving, but worse at skills that are not useful on the Internet, like deep analysis.

Tone

Informative, neutral, slightly warning

Passage 2

Passage Summary

Lines

51-59: Yes, our brain changes based on how we use it, but experience does not permanently alter our brains.

60-69: We may think we can multi–task, but really that is an illusion.

70-80: Doing one thing doesn't make you good at other things, it only makes you better at the one thing.

81-90: So, using the internet just makes you better at things on the internet. It doesn't make you worse at things that aren't on the internet.

Main Idea

Our brains learn from experience, but aren't permanently rearranged by them. Learning one thing doesn't affect how well you do other things.

Tone

Dismissive, informative

Vocabulary

Line 2	info-crunching	*a.* 정보를 대량으로 고속 처리하는
Line 6	reflex response	반사반응
Line 7	visual cue	시각 단서
Line 16	welter	*n.* (정신 없을 정도로) 엄청난 양
Line 19	assess	*v.* (특성, 자질 등을) 재다[가늠하다]
Line 22	adept	*a.* 능숙한
Line 36	underpin	*v.* (주장 등을) 뒷받침하다[근거를 대다]
Line 37	inductive	*a.* 귀납적인, 유도의
Line 40	plastic	*a.* 형태를 만들[바꾸기] 쉬운
Line 45	neuroplasticity	*n.* 신경가소성
Line 46	reverberate	*v.* 소리가 울리다; 반향[파문]을 불러일으키다
Line 48	skimming	*n.* 속독, 훑어보기
Line 57	pancreas	*n.* 췌장
Line 58	blob	*n.* (작은) 방울
Line 60	revamp	*v.* (보통 더 보기 좋도록) 개조[수리]하다
Line 63	verdict	*v.* (배심원단의) 평결
Line 63	render	*v.* (어떤 상태가 되게) 만들다[하다]
Line 68	undulating	*a.* 파도 모양[기복]을 이루는
Line 68	lane	*n.* 좁은 길
Line 75	conjugating	*a.* (동사를 수, 인칭, 시제에 따라) 다른 형태를 쓰는
Line 77	bulk up	부피를 늘리다
Line 78	calisthenics	*n.* 미용 체조
Line 79	immerse	*a.* (액체 속에) 담그다
Line 87	quick cut	화면 전환 없이 이어지는 화면 전환 기법

Questions

Q22 THING: Tone, List

Answer Key : (C)

Line 3에서 technology가 "certain cognitive skills"를 improve시킬 수 있다고 하고, "fast-paced problem solving"(line 15)을 도와준다고 한다.

Eliminate

(A) passage에서 이미 여러 가지 screen-based technology에 대한 study들을 보여줌

(B) not mentioned

(D) 좋은 점이 있다고 얘기하지만, encourage되어야 한다고 말하진 않음

Q23 THING: Line Evidence

Answer Key : (A)

22번 문제의 답인 "positive effects"가 subject로 나오는 lines를 찾아보자. Lines 3-4에서 "Certain cognitive skills are strengthened by our use of computers and the Net"이라고 한다. 즉 computers와 Internet의 좋은 점도 있다는 것을 보여준다.

Eliminate

(B), (C), (D) screen-based technology 의 단점들을 비판적으로 얘기하고 있음

Q24 THING: Main Idea

Answer Key : (B)

Line 34-38에서 screen-based technology가 "inductive analysis"와 "critical thinking"을 방해한다고 말하고, lines 47-50에서 "deeply" 생각하지 못하게 만든다고 한다.

Eliminate

(A), (C), (D) not mentioned

Q25 THING: Vocabulary

Answer Key : (C)

Lines 39-41에서 "the human brain is highly plastic; neurons and synapses change as circumstances change"라고 함 → context 상 "plastic"은 "change할 수 있다"를 의미한다.

Eliminate

(A), (B), (D) wrong meaning in context

Q26 THING: Quotes, Transition Word

Answer Key : (B)

Lines 60–65에서 speed–reading은 brain이 information을 받아들이는 방법을 바꾸지 않는다고 한다. Woody Allen이 War and Peace를 빠르게 읽고 나서 이해하지 못한 것을 example로 든다.

Eliminate

(A), (C) Tolstoy의 writing style을 싫어했고 War and Peace 읽는 것을 regret했다는 내용은 not mentioned

(D) Woody Allen에 대한 example은 multitasking과 관련 없음

Q27 THING: List

Answer Key : (D)

Lines 79–80: novelist나 scientist 같은 사람들은 자기 분야를 깊이 공부하면서 실력을 키운다고 한다.

Eliminate

(A), (C) pursue knowledge하거나 curious about other subjects할 때 take risks한다는 내용은 not mentioned

(B) passage 2에서 오히려 "accomplished people"은 "intellectual calisthenics"를 연습하지 않는다고 함 (lines 77–78)

Q28 THING: Point of View, List

Answer Key : (D)

Lines 83–90에서 media critic들이 너무 alarmist하게 글을 쓴다고 비판하고 있다. 옛날 사람들이 fierce animals를 먹으면 자기도 fierce하게 될 것이라고 착각한 것과 media critic들이 electronic media를 많이 보면 brain이 달라질 것이라고 두려워하는 것을 비교한다.

Eliminate

(A), (B), (C) ornate language, humor, nostalgia에 관한 내용은 not mentioned

Q29 THING: Main Idea, Point of View

Answer Key : (D)

Passage 1에서는 screen–based technology가 thinking deeply를 방해할 수도 있다고 한다. Passage 2에서는 그와 같은 technology media를 사용하는 것은 그렇게 큰 effects를 가져오지 않을 것이라고 한다. 즉 둘 다 electronic media가 brain에 어떤 영향을 주는지에 대해 얘기하고 있다.

Eliminate

(A), (B) too specific

(C) passage 1과 2 둘 다 increasing financial support for certain studies를 support 하고 있지 않음

Q30 THING: Contrasting Pair

Answer Key : (B)

Passage 1에서 screen-based technology가 thinking deeply를 방해할 수도 있다고 하지만, Passage 2에서는 "cognitive neuroscientists roll their eyes at such talk" (lines 53-54)하면서 그런 주장을 criticize하고 있다.

Eliminate

(A) passage 1은 clinical approach가 아님

(C), (D) passage 2는 high-level view를 가지고 있지 않음 / negative reactions를 predict하고 있지 않음

Q31 THING: Point of View

Answer Key : (C)

Passage 1에서 "every medium develops some cognitive skills at the expense of others"(lines 29-31)이라고 말한다. Passage 2에서도 "If you train people to do one thing … they get better at doing that thing, but almost nothing else"(lines 71-74) → passage 1과 passage 2 둘 다 한 부분이 improve한다고 해서 다른 부분까지 좋아지지 않는다는 것에 agree한다.

Eliminate

(A) hand-eye coordination은 Passage 2에서 not mentioned

(B) passage 1에서는 media critics들이 overreact한다는 내용 not mentioned

(D) 두 passage 모두 Internet users가 printed text/digital text 중 prefer하는 것 not mentioned

Q32 THING: Line Evidence

Answer Key : (B)

문제의 keywords인 "agree to some extent", "Michael Merzenich"가 subject로 나오는 lines를 찾아보자. Lines 41-43의 주장은 우리가 새로운 medium을 사용할 때 우리는 "different brain"을 가지게 된다는 것이었다. Passage 2에서도 어느 정도 agree한다: "Yes, every time we learn a fact or skill the wiring of the brain changes"(lines 54-56).

Eliminate

(A), (C), (D) keywords 가 나오지 않음

Passage IV. Elizabeth Cady Stanton's address

Passage Summary

Lines

1-14: We need the sixteenth amendment because society run by men is horrible.

15-30: Man has had control for a long time, and because he is dark and violent and has kept the softer, gentler voice of the woman silent, society is dark and violent.

31-47: People argue against giving women the vote because they say it will make them more masculine. The author argues that because women are dependent on men, they already have to be more masculine because they need to make men happy. Giving them the vote will make them more feminine.

48-66: These days we don't need more masculinity, we need the feminine perspective to escape these situations and move to a higher civilization.

67-78: That isn't to say that all men are bad. These "masculine tendencies" have gotten us a long way. They just are being used for bad purposes.

79-85: Which is exactly why we need the female influence, to put the power of masculine tendencies back on the right track.

Main Idea

Because men and their government are violent and oppressive, women need to be granted citizenship and keep men's destructive force in check.

Tone

Persuasive, impassioned, dramatic

Vocabulary

Line 1	amendment	*n.* (법) 등의 개정[수정]
Line 2	suffrage	*n.* 투표권, 선거권, 참정권
Line 4	stern	*a.* 엄중한, 근엄한
Line 4	aggrandizing	*a.* 확대한, 과장한
Line 5	conquest	*n.* 정복
Line 5	acquisition	*n.* 습득
Line 5	breed	*v.* 사육, 번식; 가정교육
Line 9	slaughter	*n.* (가축의) 도살[도축]

Line 10	inquisition	n. 종교 재판, 심문
Line 10	imprisonment	n. 투옥, 금고
Line 11	persecution	n. 박해, 학대
Line 11	creed	n. (종교적) 교리, 신조
Line 16	run riot	마구 날뛰다
Line 18	crush out	(~을) 부수고 나가다; 탈옥하다
Line 23	untempered	a. 조절되지 않은
Line 26	fragmentary	a. 단편적인, 부분적인
Line 29	undertake	v. 착수하다, 맡다
Line 30	sublunary	a. 현세의, 이 세상의
Line 35	disfranchise	v. 선거권을 빼앗다[박탈하다]
Line 37	dilution	n. 희석, 희박해짐
Line 39	repress	v. 참다[억누르다, 억압하다]
Line 42	foothold	n. 발판, 기반
Line 45	strip of ~	~을 빼앗다
Line 46	inalienable	a. 빼앗을 수 없는
Line 52	repression	n. 탄압, 억압
Line 53	appalled	a. 오싹해진, 질겁한
Line 54	excess	n. 지나침, 과도, 과잉
Line 54	mourn	v. 애도하다, 슬퍼하다
Line 57	specie	n. 정금, 정화(주화)
Line 57	evangel	n. 복음, (복음 같은) 희소식
Line 58	exalt	v. 승격, 격상시키다
Line 61	enfranchisement	n. 참정[선거]권 부여
Line 65	usher	n. 안내하다, 도입하다
Line 75	expend	v. (많은 시간, 돈, 에너지를) 쏟다
Line 77	subjugate	v. 예속시키다, 지배[통제] 하에 두다
Line 79	conservator	n. 관리자, 관리위원
Line 80	assert	v. (강하게) 주장하다

Questions

Q33 THING: Main Idea, Problem

Answer Key : (B)

Lines 16–31: 남자들이 모든 decision들을 내려서 society가 "fragmentary"하고 disorganized하다고 한다. 즉 여자들이 decision 내리는 것을 돕지 못해서 societal breakdown이 일어나고 있다고 한다.

Second best answer: (C)

Women이 vote하지 못한 것을 imply했지만, 그 대신 "poor candidates"가 election들을 이겼다고 말하지 않음

Eliminate

(A), (D) women이 equal educational opportunities / ability to hold political positions를 가지지 못했다는 내용이 focus는 아님

(C) "poor candidates"가 election을 이겼다는 내용 없음

Q34 THING: Main Idea, Tone

Answer Key : (A)

"High carnival"을 사용하면서 남자들이 power를 혼자 너무 많이 가지고 있어서 여자들이 repress되었다고 한다.

Eliminate

(B), (C), (D) time period가 unrestricted함, scandalous decline in moral values, power of women is growing하다는 내용과 관련 없음

Q35 THING: Contrasting Pair

Answer Key : (D)

Lines 21–22에서 womanhood가 "scrace been recognized as a power until within the last century"이라고 하므로 womanhood는 최근에 인정된 power라는 것을 알 수 있다.

Eliminate

(A), (B), (C) 모두 오래 전부터 있었던 것들임

Q36 THING: Line Evidence

Answer Key : (B)

35번 문제의 keyword인 "recent historical development", "women's true character"가 나오는 lines를 찾아보자. Lines 16–23에서 womanhood가 "scarce been recognized as a power until within the last century"라고 한다.

Eliminate

(A), (C), (D) keyword가 나오지 않음

Q37 THING: Vocabulary

Answer Key : (B)

Lines 23-26에서 "Society is but the reflection of man himself ... the hard iron rule we feel alike in the church, the state, and the home"이라고 함 → "rule"한다는 것은 사회 모든 부분에서 control한다는 의미이다.

Eliminate

(A), (C), (D) wrong meaning in context

Q38 THING: Tone, Quotes

Answer Key : (D)

Lines 32-35에서 사람들이 "strong-minded"라는 단어를 vote하기 위해서 노력하는 여자들한테 apply한다고 한다. 즉 strong-minded라는 단어로 female suffragists를 criticize하려고 한다.

Eliminate

(A), (B) "strong-minded"가 여기서 칭찬으로 사용되고 있지 않음
(C) criticize하는 것은 맞지만, male professions에 들어가는 것보다 vote하는 것과 더 관련이 많음

Q39 THING: Vocabulary

Answer Key : (C)

Lines 36-39에서 "best sense"의 여자들이 society에 없다고 하면서, 대부분의 여자들은 남자들의 "reflections, varieties, and dilutions"라고 비판한다. 즉 여기에서 "best"는 남자의 reflections 등이 아닌, "genuine"을 의미한다.

Eliminate

(A), (B), (D) incorrect in context

Q40 THING: Problem, List

Answer Key : (A)

Lines 54-56에서 남자도 "mourn"하면서 자신의 power가 "falsehood, selfishness, and violence"를 만든 것에 대해서 슬퍼한다고 한다. 즉 남자들도 자기의 control이 만드는 문제들에 대해서 regret한다고 말한다.

Eliminate

(B), (C), (D) 남자들이 advocating for women's right to vote/female equality, requesting women's opinions about improvising civic life한다는 것에 대한 내용 not mentioned

Q41 THING: Line Evidence

Answer Key : (B)

40번 문제의 keywords인 "dire", "lament", "problems"가 나오는 lines를 찾아보자. Lines 54–56의 "appalled", "excesses" 등이 keyword의 synonym이 될 수 있다. 이를 통해 남자들도 상황을 regret하는 내용을 보여준다.

Eliminate

(A), (C), (D) keywords가 나오지 않음

Q42 THING: Contrasting Pair

Answer Key : (D)

Lines 67–68에서 남자들은 무조건 나쁜 것은 아니라는 것을 강조하면서, masculine trait들 중에서 잘못 쓰이면 나빠지는 것이라고 설명을 하고 있다.

Eliminate

(A), (B) sixth paragraph는 contrast between men and women / spiritual and material worlds 와 관련 없음

(C) 남자들이 다 나쁜 것은 아니라고 하지만 "good" man을 constitute하는 것이 무엇인지에 대해서는 explain하지 않음

Passage V.   "Long a Mystery, How 500-Meter-High Undersea ..."

Passage Summary

Lines
1-11: You can't see them, but underwater ocean waves are huge and important.
12-19: They move heat around the world so they influence global climate, but many climate models don't incorporate them. They should incorporate underwater waves in order to be accurate.
20-28: Peacock and his colleagues are tracking what are thought to be the biggest internal waves in the world in Taiwan and the Philippines.
29-41: They built a giant facility to simulate the creation of these waves because we don't understand them yet.
42-52: They recreated the Luzon strait completely, including the water salinity levels and the shape of the ocean floor.
53-64: The unique shape of the floor in combination with the motion of the tides causes the internal waves. They act like above ground waves, just underwater, breaking against the shore.
65-end: The info is specific to the Luzon strait, but it is applicable all over the world, and will result in more accurate climate analysis because of how important they are to climate.

Main Idea

We are finding out more about internal waves thanks to research, and that is good for climate science.

Tone

Informative, enthusiastic

Vocabulary

Line 5	undetectable	a. 감지할 수 없는
Line 10	staggering	a. (너무 엄청나서) 충격적인, 믿기 어려운
Line 11	skyscraper	n. 고층 건물
Line 37	diameter	n. 지름, 직경
Line 41	oceanographic	a. 해양학의
Line 42	resin	n. 수지, 송진

Line 44	topography	n. 지형, 지형학
Line 45	salinity	n. 염분, 염도
Line 48	briny	a. 물이 짠, 염분이 많은
Line 51	plunger	n. 고무판(피스톤 같은 것을 밀어내리도록 되어 있는)
Line 54	double-ridge	a. 이중으로 솟아오른
Line 59	trailed	a. 뒤따르는
Line 65	devise	v. 창안[고안]하다

Questions

Q43 THING: Main Idea

Answer Key : (C)

Line 3에서 "internal waves"를 mention한 후, lines 7–9에서는 "transferring heat to the ocean depths and bringing up cold water from below"라고 하면서 internal waves가 왜 중요한지 얘기한다.

Eliminate

(A), (B), (D) paragraph는 scientific device, common misconception, recent study에 focus하고 있지 않음

Q44 THING: Vocabulary

Answer Key : (B)

Lines 17–19에서 정확한 global climate model을 만들려면 internal waves가 만들어지는 process를 capture해야 한다고 함 → context 상 "capture"는 scientific study를 위해서 record한다는 뜻이다.

Eliminate

(A), (C), (D) wrong meaning in context

Q45 THING: Quotes

Answer Key : (D)

Lines 17–19에서 Tom Peacock은 과학자들은 internal waves에 대해서 더 많이 공부해서 더 정확한 climate models를 만들어야 한다고 한다. 즉 internal waves에 대해서 공부를 하면 scientific models를 만드는데 도움이 될 것이라고 주장한다.

Eliminate

(A), (B), (C) monitoring internal waves가 verify wave heights, improve satellite image quality, prevent coastal damage를 allow할 것이라는 내용은 not mentioned

Q46 THING: Line Evidence

Answer Key : (C)

45번 문제의 keywords인 "Peacock", "ability to monitor internal waves", "significant", "key scientific models"가 subject로 나오는 lines를 찾아보자. Lines 17–19에서 Tom Peacock은 internal waves에 대해서 공부하면 "more and more accurate climate models"를 만들 수 있을 것이라고 한다.

Eliminate

(A), (B), (D) keywords가 나오지 않음

Q47 THING: Vocabulary

Answer Key : (A)

Lines 65–67에서 Tom Peacock와 그의 team이 "were able to devise a mathematical model that describes ... these waves" 라고 함 → context 상 "devise"는 mathematical model을 create한다는 뜻이다.

Eliminate

(B), (C), (D) incorrect in context

Q48 THING: Main Idea, Problem

Answer Key : (B)

Lines 53–55에서 topography의 double-ridge shape가 "generating the underwater [internal] waves"한다고 한다. 즉 topography 차이로 달라질 수 있다.

Eliminate

(A) line 25에서 Luzon Strait에 있는 internal waves는 "some of the largest in the world"라고 하는 것을 보아, 항상 높이가 똑같다고 말할 수 없음

(C), (D) researchers' findings가 support하는 내용이 아님

Q49 THING: Line Evidence

Answer Key : (D)

48번 문제의 keywords인 'internal waves", "distinct topographies", "different regions"가 subject로 나오는 lines를 찾아보자. Lines 67–70에서 internal waves가 topography로 영향 받는다는 것을 말한 후, 그런 발견들로 인해서 "help researchers understand how internal waves are generated in other places around the world"라고 한다. 즉 모든 internal waves가 비슷한 이유로 영향 받는다는 것을 알 수 있다.

Eliminate

(A), (B), (C) keywords가 나오지 않음

Q50 THING: Graph

Answer Key : (D)

Graph에서는 19:12–20:24 사이에 13×C isotherm의 깊이가 20m에서 40m로 커진다.

Eliminate

(A), (B), (C) not supported by graph: 여기서 나온 isotherm들은 다 깊이가 줄어들었음

Q51 THING: Graph

Answer Key : (D)

Lines 3–6에서 internal wave들은 surface에 있지 않고 바다 밑에서 움직인다고 말한다. Graph에서도 isotherm들의 depth가 0이 되지 않는 것을 보면, surface에 나타나지 않는다는 것을 support한다.

Eliminate

(A) graph에서 salinity에 대한 내용은 없음

(B), (C) not supported by graph

Q52 THING: Graph

Answer Key : (A)

Graph에서 internal wave 때문에 warm isotherm들이 원래 cold한 깊이로 가게 하는 것을 보여준다.

Eliminate

(B), (C), (D) not shown in graph

Section 2. Writing and Language Test

Q1
Answer : (B)
Category : Vocabulary
Explanation
  "cuts"와 같은 "감소"라는 뜻의 "reductions"를 써야 한다. 정답은 (B)
Eliminate
  (A) gerund form인 "reducing"보다 noun인 "reductions"이 더 정확함
  (B) "deducting"과 "deducts"의 뜻은 "공제하다"

Q2
Answer : (B)
Category : Vocabulary
Explanation
  "public libraries"의 "operating funds"가 reduced된 이후 result를 이야기하는 다음 문장으로 transtion하는 conjunctive adverb가 필요하다. 정답은 (B)
Eliminate
  (A), (C) contradiction의 뜻의 conjunctive adverb
  (C) 이후 result를 이야기함

Q3
Answer : (A)
Category : SVD, Incomplete Sentences
Explanation
  문장의 subject인 "trend"가 singular이기 때문에 singular form verb가 필요하다. 정답은 (A)
Eliminate
  (B) plural form verb
  (C), (D) verb가 없는 sentence fragment가 됨

Q4
Answer : (A)
Category : Insert/Delete/Replace
Explanation
  "nonprint formats"의 examples를 provide하는 문장이므로 필요하다. 정답은 (A)
Eliminate
  (B) 다음 문장과 관련 없음
  (C), (D) 문장을 더 clear하게 만들어주기 때문에 필요함

Q5
Answer : (D)
Category : Wordiness
Explanation
  가장 concise하고 clear해야 한다. 정답은 (D)
Eliminate
  (A), (B), (C) too wordy

Q6
Answer : (D)
Category : Parallelism
Explanation
  "compiling", "updating"과 parallel해야 한다. 정답은 (D)
Eliminate
  (A), (B), (C) "catalog", "librarians cataloging", "to catalog"는 "compiling"과 "updating"과 parallel하지 않음

Q7

Answer : (B)

Category : Wordiness, Incomplete Sentences

Explanation

"librarians"들이 하는 일에 focus하며 두 문장을 가장 concise한 문장으로 combine해야 한다. 정답은 (B)

Eliminate

(A), (C), (D) wordy하고 원래 문장의 뜻과 맞지 않음

Q8

Answer : (D)

Category : Redundancy

Explanation

"while"은 문장의 시작에 쓰는 conjunction으로 comma 뒤에 나오는 clause를 contradict하기 때문에 but이 필요 없다. 정답은 (D)

Eliminate

(A), (B), (C) 이미 conjunction이 있음

Q9

Answer : (B)

Category : Insert/Delete/Replace

Explanation

"free resources"가 "valuable"한 것이므로 expensive resources를 afford할 수 없을 때에 관한 information이 나와야 한다. 정답은 (B)

Eliminate

(A), (C), (D) 문장과 관련 없음

Q10

Answer : (B)

Category : Wordiness, Register

Explanation

"law"와 관련된 문제를 가장 concise하고 clear하게 express해야 한다. 정답은 (B)

Eliminate

(A) too informal

(C), (D) too wordy

Q11

Answer : (C)

Category : Insert/Delete/Replace

Explanation

"technological advances"가 어떻게 "librarians"의 role을 change했는지 설명하는 passage를 summarize하는 문장이 필요하다. 정답은 (C)

Eliminate

(A), (B), (D) passage의 main point와 관련 없음

Q12

Answer : (B)

Category : Vocabulary

Explanation

"famous large paintings"의 example을 provide하는 다음 문장으로 transition하는 phrase가 필요하다. 정답은 (B)

Eliminate

(A), (C), (D) example을 provide하는 transitional phrase가 아님

Q13

Answer : (D)

Category : Various Comma Usages

Explanation

"painter . . . Jatte"가 문장의 object clause이고 중간에 "painter George Seurat's"는 additional information이 아니기 때문에 전후에 comma를 사용할 수 없다. 정답은 (D)

Eliminate

(A), (B), (C) comma 사용할 수 없음

Q14

Answer : (C)
Category : Colons and Dashes, Diction
Explanation
 "favorite exhibit"이 무엇인지 introduce하는 punctuation이 필요하다. 정답은 (C)
Eliminate
 (A), (B), (D) transition이 아니므로 semi-colon을 쓸 수 없고 it's는 possessive pronoun이 아닌 "it is"의 contraction임

Q15

Answer : (C)
Category : Insert/Delete/Replace
Explanation
 "rooms"의 decorations에 관한 passage이므로 "French Revolution"에 관한 문장이 불필요하다. 정답은 (C)
Eliminate
 (A), (B), (C) passage와 관련 없음

Q16

Answer : (C)
Category : Conjunction Errors - General
Explanation
 두 개의 independent clause를 conjunction을 사용해서 연결해야 한다. 정답은 (C)
Eliminate
 (A), (B) conjunction이 없이 두 개의 independent clause가 있음
 (D) sentence fragment

Q17

Answer : (B)
Category : Parallelism
Explanation
 length unit인 "inches"를 "couch" measurement로 사용했으므로 같은 unit으로 measure한 것이 와야 한다. 정답은 (B)
Eliminate
 (A) 같은 unit이 아님
 (C) clear하지 않음
 (D) example이 아님

Q18

Answer : (B)
Category : Conjunction Errors - General
Explanation
 "plainer rooms"가 "sparsely furnished"하지만, details가 더 "true to the periods"하다고 transition해 주는 conjunction이 필요하다. 정답은 (B)
Eliminate
 (A) preposition은 independent clauses를 connect할 수 없음
 (C) 두 문장의 relationship를 보여주지 않음
 (D) "whereas"는 다른 두 가지 사실을 비교할 때 사용하지만, 이 문장에서는 "plainer rooms"에 대해서만 이야기하고 있음

Q19

Answer : (A)
Category : Parallelism
Explanation
 Noun phrase들과 parallel해야 한다. 정답은 (A)
Eliminate
 (B), (C), (D) subject와 verb가 있는 clause이기 때문에 previous examples와 parallel하지 않음

Q20

Answer : (D)

Category : Various Comma Usages, Number Agreement

Explanation

quote 전에 quote의 주인과 verb가 와야 하고, [overhear + object + infitinive or –ing] grammar rule을 따라야 한다. 정답은 (D)

Eliminate

(A) comma가 뒤에 있기 때문에 noun이 올 수 없음

(B) article이 "a"이기 때문에 singular noun이 와야함

(C) [overhear + object + infitinive or –ing] rule에 따라서 past tense verb가 올 수 없음

Q21

Answer : (D)

Category : Front Modifier

Explanation

"dotted with pin–sized knobs"는 "visitor"가 아닌 "drawers"를 modify하는 것이므로 front에 올 수 없다. 정답은 (D)

Eliminate

(A), (B), (C) "dotted with pin–sized knobs"는 "visitor"를 modify하지 않음

Q22

Answer : (B)

Category : Content Order

Explanation

"Thorne Miniature Rooms"를 introduce하는 것으로 끝나는 paragraph 1 뒤에 "miniature rooms"를 describe하는 paragraph 3가 와야 하며, 그 뒤에 더 specific한 example인 "intricate"한 room에 관한 내용을 담은 paragraph 2가 와야 한다. 그리고 마지막에 "more sparsely furnished rooms"에 관한 paragraph 4가 와야 한다. 정답은 (B)

Eliminate

(A), (C), (D) passage의 흐름에 맞지 않음

Q23

Answer : (A)

Category : Incomplete Sentences

Explanation

Subject "sea otters"의 verb는 "help"이므로 중간에 subjective pronoun이나 conjunction을 쓸 수 없다. 정답은 (A)

Eliminate

(B), (C), (D) sentence fragment

Q24

Answer : (B)

Category : Graph

Explanation

그래프의 내용을 가장 잘 나타낸 답은 (B)

Eliminate

(A) Two years or less인 경우, sea urchin들이 많이 줄어들 수는 있지만 전부 사라지지는 않음

(C), (D) not supported by graph

Q25

Answer : (B)

Category : Vocabulary

Explanation

"sea otters"의 presence가 어떻게 "kelp forests"를 affect하는지 discuss하는 앞 문장에서 "sea otters"의 presence가 없으면 반대로 어떻게 negative하게 change하는지 설명하는 문장으로 transition하는 conjunctive adverb가 필요하다. 정답은 (B)

Eliminate

(A) "nevertheless"의 뜻은 "그렇기는 하지만"이라는 뜻이기 때문에 앞 문장도 뒷 문장과 같이 negative해야 함

(C), (D) contradiction의 뜻의 conjunctive adverb가 아님

Q26

Answer : (A)

Category : Insert/Delete/Replace

Explanation

앞 문장에서 discuss한 "global warming"과 "carbon dioxide"가 어떤 relationship이 있는지 establish하기 때문에 필요하다. 정답은 (A)

Eliminate

(B) "sea otters, sea urchins, and kelp forests"와 관계 없음

(C), (D) 문장의 purpose를 clarify하므로 필요함

Q27

Answer : (D)

Category : Various Comma Usages

Explanation

"that [...] kelp"는 object clause이므로 verb 바로 뒤에 punctuation 없이 나와야 한다. 정답은 (D)

Eliminate

(A), (B), (C) punctuation 불필요

Q28

Answer : (A)

Category : Vocabulary

Explanation

"sea urchins"가 "kelp"를 "잡아먹는다"는 뜻의 단어가 필요하다. 정답은 (A)

Eliminate

(B) "dispatch"의 뜻은 "죽이다"

(C) "overindulge one"의 뜻은 "탐닉하다"

(D) "dispose of"의 뜻은 "~을 없애다"

Q29

Answer : (C)

Category : Number agreement

Explanation

singular noun인 "kelp"의 "terrestrial plant cousins"이므로 third person singular possessive pronoun을 써야 한다. 정답은 (C)

Eliminate

(A) plural pronoun

(B) "they are"의 contraction

(C) "it is"의 contraction

Q30

Answer : (C)

Category : Ambiguous Pronoun

Explanation

Subjective pronoun의 antecedent가 clear하지 않으므로 "sea otters"라고 다시 mention해야 한다. 정답은 (C)

Eliminate

(A), (B), (D) pronoun이 무엇을 refer하는지 clear하지 않음

Q31

Answer : (D)

Category : Insert/Delete/Replace

Explanation

전에 알지 못하던 사실을 알아서 "surprised"됐다는 내용이므로 "scientists"들이 "how large a role sea otters played"를 몰랐다는 내용의 sentence 5 뒤에 와야 한다. 정답은 (D)

Eliminate

(A), (B), (C) passage의 흐름을 방해함

Q32

Answer : (B)

Category : Register

Explanation

　Scientific passage에 맞는 vocabulary를 사용해서 "otter의 개체수가 증가한다"는 expression을 사용해야 한다. 정답은 (B)

Eliminate

　(A), (C), (D) informal, unclear

Q33

Answer : (D)

Category : Various Comma Usages

Explanation

　"sequestered"와 "removed"는 interchangeable한 표현으로 둘 다 사용할 수 있는 additional information이기 때문에 "or removed" 전후에 comma가 와야 한다. 정답은 (D)

Eliminate

　(A) sentence fragment

　(B), (C) additional information은 "or removed"

Q34

Answer : (D)

Category : Pronoun Shift

Explanation

　"practice가 ~하는"이라는 뜻의 pronoun을 써야 한다. practice, method, system 등의 표현과 가장 많이 쓰이는 pronoun은 whereby. 정답은 (D)

Eliminate

　(A), (B), (C) incorrect pronoun

Q35

Answer : (A)

Category : Various Comma Usages

Explanation

　"a practice [...] usefulness"는 "planned obsolescence"의 additional information이기 때문에 전후에 comma가 와야 한다. 정답은 (A)

Eliminate

　(B) additional information 전에 dash가 없음

　(C) sentence fragment

　(D) additional information 끝에 comma가 필요함

Q36

Answer : (D)

Category : Vocabulary

Explanation

　"contrast"를 modify하는 adjective이므로 차이가 "극명한"이라는 뜻의 단어가 와야 한다. 정답은 (D)

Eliminate

　(A) "austere"의 뜻은 "소박한"

　(B) "egregious"의 뜻은 "지독한"

　(C) "unmitigated"의 뜻은 "완전한"

Q37

Answer : (A)

Category : Insert/Delete/Replace

Explanation

　"belief that it is easier to replace goods than to mend them"의 이유를 provide하는 것이므로 "repair shops are rare"와 비슷한 다른 이유가 필요하다. 정답은 (A)

Eliminate

　(B), (C), (D) 문장과 관련 없음

Q38

Answer : (B)
Category : Diction
Explanation
"actual cafe"보다 박람회 같았다는 뜻의 문장이므로, "박람회"라는 뜻의 "fair"와 "~보다"라는 뜻의 "than"이 필요하다. 정답은 (B)
Eliminate
(A), (C), (D) "fare"의 뜻은 "요금", "then"의 뜻은 "그 다음에"

Q39

Answer : (C)
Category : Conjunction Errors - General
Explanation
"Martine Postma"에 대해 설명하는 subordinate clause의 subject form에 맞는 subordinating conjunction인 who를 써야 한다. 정답은 (C)
Eliminate
(A), (D) conjunction이 없음
(B) "whom"은 objective form

Q40

Answer : (D)
Category : Vocabulary
Explanation
Transition이 필요하지 않기 때문에 conjunctive adverb도 필요 없다. 정답은 (D)
Eliminate
(A), (B), (D) conjunctive adverb 불필요

Q41

Answer : (D)
Category : Front Modifier, Redundancy
Explanation
"While [...] service"는 patrons를 modify하는 front modifier이기 때문에 subject와 conjugated verb는 필요 없다. 정답은 (D)

Eliminate
(A), (B), (C) subject와 conjugated verb 필요 없음, "wait for"와 "await"는 synonymous

Q42

Answer : (C)
Category : Insert/Delete/Replace
Explanation
"first Repair Cafe"의 influence를 describe하는 내용이므로 "Martine Postma"가 "first Repair Cafe"로 어떤 changes를 만들려고 했는지 describe하는 내용을 담은 sentence 3 뒤에 와야 한다. 정답은 (C)
Eliminate
(A), (B), (D) passage의 흐름을 방해함

Q43

Answer : (C)
Category : Insert/Delete/Replace
Explanation
Passage의 전후 문장과 관련 없다. 정답은 (C)
Eliminate
(A), (B), (C) 관련 없는 내용으로 passage의 흐름을 방해함

Q44

Answer : (D)
Category : Wordiness, Redundancy
Explanation
"other"가 있으므로 다른 비슷한 뜻의 expression이 필요 없다.
Eliminate
(A), (B), (C) "on top of that", "in addition", "likewise"는 "other..." 와 similar해서 wordy함

Section 3. Math Test
(No Calculator)

Q1
Answer : (C)
Category : Equations
Explanation
$5x+6=100$이므로
$5x=4 \to 10x=8 \to 10x+3=11$
∴ C

Q2
Answer : (B)
Category : Equations
Explanation
System of Linear Equations를 풀면
$x+y=0$ ……①
$3x-2y=10$ ……②
①×2+②=$5x=10 \to x=2, y=-2$
∴ B

Q3
Answer : (A)
Category : Equations
Explanation
Price가 $60+12nh$이고 n이 landscapers 수, h가 total number of hours이므로 "12"는 각 landscaper의 수당인 것이 가장 logical하다.
∴ A

Q4
Answer : (A)
Category : Factoring
Explanation
$9a^4+12a^2b^2+4b^4$
$=(3a^2)^2+2(3a^2)(2b^2)+(2b^2)^2$
$=(3a^2+2b^2)^2$
∴ A

Q5
Answer : (C)
Category : Powers and Roots
Explanation
$\sqrt{(2k^2+17)}-x=0, x=7$
$\to \sqrt{(2k^2+17)}=7$
$\to 2k^2+17=49$
$\to k^2=16$
$k>0$이므로 $k=4$
∴ C

Q6
Answer : (D)
Category : Functions
Explanation
Parallel하므로 slope가 같다.
Slope of line $l=\dfrac{0-(-5)}{2-0}=\dfrac{5}{2}$
Slope of line $k=\dfrac{p-0}{0-(-4)}=\dfrac{p}{4}$
$\dfrac{5}{2}=\dfrac{p}{4} \to p=10$
∴ D

Q7
Answer : (A)
Category : Powers and Roots, Equations
Explanation
$\dfrac{x^{a^2}}{x^{b^2}}=x^{16} \to x^{a^2}=x^{(16+b^2)}$
∴ $a^2=16+b^2 \to (a-b)(a+b)=16$
$a+b=20$이므로 $a-b=8$
∴ A

Q8

Answer : (C)

Category : Polygons, Equations

Explanation

$nA = 360$

$A = \dfrac{360}{n} > 50°$

$360 > 50n \rightarrow 7.2 > n$

가장 큰 $n = 7$이므로

∴ C

Q9

Answer : (B)

Category : Functions

Explanation

첫 번째 graph는 slope가 2이고 $(1, 8)$를 지나므로

$y - 8 = 2(x - 1) \rightarrow y = 2x + 6$

두 번째 graph는 $(1, 2)$와 $(2, 1)$을 지나므로

$y - 1 = \dfrac{1-2}{2-1}(x - 2) \rightarrow y = -x + 3$

Intersection $= (a, b)$이므로

$2x + 6 = -x + 3 \rightarrow x = -1, y = 4$

$a + b = 3$

∴ B

Q10

Answer : (C)

Category : Functions

Explanation

y의 value가 -1보다 항상 커야 하는데

(A), (B), (D)는 각각 y-intercept가 -2이다.

따라서 항상 y의 value가 -2일 때가 있다는 것이다.

(C)에서 항상 $y = (x-2)^2 \geq 0 > -1$이므로

∴ C

Q11

Answer : (C)

Category : Numbers

Explanation

$\dfrac{3-5i}{8+2i} = \dfrac{3-5i}{8+2i} \times \dfrac{8-2i}{8-2i} = \dfrac{(3-5i)(8-2i)}{64+16i-16i+4}$

$\dfrac{24-40i-6i-10}{68} = \dfrac{14-46i}{68} = \dfrac{7-23i}{34}$

∴ C

Q12

Answer : (B)

Category : Equations

Explanation

$R = \dfrac{F}{N+F} \rightarrow RN + RF = F$

$\rightarrow F(1 - R) = RN$

$\rightarrow F = \dfrac{RN}{1-R}$

∴ B

Q13

Answer : (D)

Category : Equations

Explanation

$2m^2 - 16m + 8 = 0$

$\rightarrow m^2 - 8m + 4 = 0$

Sum of two roots $= -\dfrac{-8}{1} = 8$

∴ D

Q14

Answer : (A)

Category : Functions

Explanation

Annual decay rate $= 13\%$ 이므로

Remaining amount after 1 year $= 325 \times 0.87$g

after 2 years $= (325 \times 0.87) \times 0.87 = 325 \times 0.87^2$

after t years $= 325 \times 0.87^t$

∴ A

Q15

Answer : (D)

Category : Divisibility, Fractions

Explanation

$$\frac{5x-2}{x+3} = \frac{5x+15-17}{x+3} = \frac{5(x+3)-17}{x+3}$$
$$= 5 - \frac{17}{x+3}$$

∴ D

Q16

Answer : 3, 6, or 9

Category : Numbers, Divisibility

Explanation

$750를 받는 사람 수를 x, $250를 받는 사람 수를 y라고 하면,

$750x + 250y = 3{,}000 \quad (x, y \geq 1, \ x, y \in Z)$

$\rightarrow 3x + y = 12$

x, y가 integer이므로 $y = 3, 6, 9$

∴ 3, 6, or 9

Q17

Answer : 19

Category : Equations

Explanation

$2x(3x+5) + 3(3x+5)$

$\rightarrow 6x^2 + 10x + 9x + 15$

$\quad = 6x^2 + 19x + 15 = ax^2 + bx + c$

True for all values of x이므로 $b = 19$

∴ 19

Q18

Answer : 12

Category : Triangles

Explanation

$\overline{AE} \parallel \overline{CD}$이므로 $\triangle ABE \sim \triangle DBC$

$\overline{BC} : \overline{BE} = \overline{BD} : \overline{BA} = 1 : 2$

$\overline{BC} = 4$이므로 $\overline{CE} = \overline{BC} + \overline{BE} = 12$

∴ 12

Q19

Answer : 6

Category : Trigonometry

Explanation

$\overline{OA} = \sqrt{(\sqrt{3})^2 + 1^2} = 2$

$\sin \angle AOB = \frac{1}{2}$이므로

$\angle AOB = 30° = \frac{\pi}{a}$ rad

∴ $a = 6$

Q20

Answer : $\frac{1}{4}$ or .25

Category : Equations

Explanation

$ax + by = 12$

$2x + 8y = 60$

Infinitely many solutions이므로

$\frac{a}{2} = \frac{b}{8} = \frac{12}{60}$

$8a = 2b \rightarrow 4a = b \rightarrow \frac{a}{b} = \frac{1}{4}$

∴ $\frac{1}{4}$ or .25

Section 4. Math Test
(Calculator)

Q1
Answer : (C)
Category : Equations
Explanation
Download가 d번 되었으므로 $0.09 \times d$,
streaming이 s번 되었으므로 $0.002 \times s$
∴ C

Q2
Answer : (B)
Category : Ratio
Explanation
400개마다 7개를 inspect한다고 했으므로
$400 : 7 = 20000 : x \rightarrow x = 350$
∴ B

Q3
Answer : (A)
Category : Equations
Explanation
$l = 24 + 3.5m$, $l = 73$
$\rightarrow 73 = 24 + 3.5m \rightarrow m = 14$
∴ A

Q4
Answer : (C)
Category : Ratio
Explanation
Directly proportional하게 pay를 받는다고 했으므로 $120 : 8 = x : 20 \rightarrow x = 300$
∴ C

Q5
Answer : (C)
Category : Percentage
Explanation
Profit = Total revenue − Total cost
$= 100 - 43 = 57\%$ of total revenue
$= 120 \times 0.57 = \$68.40$
∴ C

Q6
Answer : (B)
Category : Equations
Explanation
$4x + 12 = 8 \rightarrow x = -1$
$2x + 7 = -2 + 7 = 5$
∴ B

Q7
Answer : (D)
Category : Functions
Explanation
$y = x^2 - 6x + 8 = (x-2)(x-4)$
x−intercept는 y의 value를 0으로 만드는 value이므로 위의 form으로 나타내면 x−intercept를 알 수 있다.
∴ D

Q8
Answer : (D)
Category : Equations
Explanation
Task를 complete하지 않으면 2 points를 k에서 뺀다. 100개의 task를 complete하지 않았으므로 total points $= k - 2 \times 100 = 200 \rightarrow k = 400$
∴ D

Q9

Answer : (A)

Category : Equations

Explanation

Forklift가 최대 2400 pounds, 45 box를 carry할 수 있다고 했으므로
$40x+65y \leq 2400$
$x+y \leq 45$
∴ A

Q10

Answer : (B)

Category : Functions

Explanation

$f(2)=3$, $f(3)=5$
$g(3)=2$, $g(5)=6$
$f(g(3))=f(2)=3$
∴ B

Q11

Answer : (B)

Category : Graphs and Data Analysis

Explanation

Table에서 significant한 information만 골라보면,
Number of hours Tony plans to read per day$=3$
Number of words Tony reads per minute$=250$
Number of words in the novel$=349,168$
3 hours$=180$ minutes 이므로
Number of words Tony reads per DAY
$=180 \times 250=45,000$
Number of days it takes Tony to read the novel$=349,168 \div 45,000 \cong 7.76 \cong 8$ days
∴ B

Q12

Answer : (D)

Category : Equations

Explanation

1 year마다 7,500 tons씩 증가하면 total increase$=7,500y$ tons이다. At or above capacity라고 했으므로
$175,000+7,500y \geq 325,000$
∴ D

Q13

Answer : (D)

Category : Graphs and Data Analysis

Explanation

Data를 분석할 때 실질적인 "numbers"에 관련된 variable이 아닌 것은 data에 영향을 주지 않는다.
(A) Sample size, (B) Population size, (C) Number of people who refused는 전부 data size에 영향을 주기 때문에 data reliability에 영향을 준다.
(D) "where"는 data size에 irrelevant하기 때문에 data reliability에 영향을 주지 않는다.
∴ D

Q14

Answer : (C)

Category : Graphs and Data Analysis

Explanation

Line of best fit에서 550 billion miles인 coordinate을 찾아보면 2000년과 2005년 사이에 있음을 볼 수 있다.
∴ C

Q15

Answer : (A)

Category : Ratio, Rate

Explanation

580,000,000 miles를 1 year에 travel 했으므로 이것을 miles per HOUR로 계산하면,

$$\frac{580,000,000}{365 \times 24} \cong 66,210 \cong 66,000$$

∴ A

Q16

Answer : (B)

Category : Probability, Graphs and Data Analysis

Explanation

Probability

$= \dfrac{\text{Graduates who did not take review course}}{\text{Total number of Graduates who passed the bar}}$

$= \dfrac{7}{25}$

∴ B

Q17

Answer : (C)

Category : Percentage

Explanation

Amu가 20% less라고 했으므로

$40 \times 0.8 = 32$

∴ C

Q18

Answer : (C)

Category : Statistics

Explanation

Mean이 165,000이고 Median이 125,000이다. 만약 survey data값 전체를 크기 순으로 나열했을 때 distribution이 균등하게 되어 있다면 mean과 median의 value가 같아야 한다. 하지만 mean이 median보다 크므로 value가 매우 큰 data 값이 몇몇 존재하여 mean을 높여놓은 것이라고 해석할 수 있다.

∴ C

Q19

Answer : (B)

Category : Statistics, Graphs and Data Analysis

Explanation

Lincoln School과 Washington School 전부의 median값을 구해야 한다.

총 600명의 data를 나열하여 가장 중간 값을 구하려면 300번째 data값과 301번째 data값을 봐야 한다. 첫 260명은 0으로 나열되고 나머지 40명을 다음 range에서 채워 넣을 수 있다. 따라서 다음 40명은 1의 range에 속한다.

∴ B

Q20

Answer : (C)

Category : Ratio, Graphs and Data Analysis

Explanation

Survey가 총 300명씩 각 학교에서 random으로 sampling을 한 것이므로 절대적인 data값을 보기보다는 그 ratio를 봐야 한다.

Lincoln School은 2,400명 중 300명을 survey한 것이므로 $10 \times \dfrac{300}{2400} = 80$

Washington School은 3,300명 중 300명을 survey한 것이므로 $10 \times \dfrac{300}{3300} = 110$

따라서 30명의 차이가 나게 된다.

∴ C

Q21

Answer : (D)

Category : Equations, Absolute Value

Explanation

Within 10hours of the time it actually takes 라고 했으므로 $|y-x| < 10$이 되어야 한다.

→ $-10 < y-x < 10$

∴ D

Q22

Answer : (B)

Category : Equations

Explanation

$I = \dfrac{P}{4\pi r^2} \rightarrow 4\pi r^2 = \dfrac{P}{I} \rightarrow r^2 = \dfrac{P}{4\pi I}$

∴ B

Q23

Answer : (A)

Category : Ratio, Equations

Explanation

Intensity가 16 times라고 했는데 P가 일정하다. 따라서 r에 따라 Intensity가 결정된다.

$I \propto \dfrac{1}{r^2}$ 이므로 r^2은 $\dfrac{1}{4^2}$, r은 $\dfrac{1}{4}$이 된다.

∴ A

Q24

Answer : (A)

Category : Circle Equation

Explanation

$x^2 + y^2 + 4x - 2y = -1$
$(x^2 + 4x + 4) - 4 + (y^2 - 2y + 1) - 1 = -1$
$(x+2)^2 + (y-1)^2 = 2^2$ 이므로

∴ A

Q25

Answer : (A)

Category : Functions

Explanation

Slope $= \dfrac{b-0}{0-a} = -\dfrac{b}{a}$

$a + b = 0 \rightarrow a = -b$

∴ slope $= -\dfrac{b}{a} = -\dfrac{b}{-b} = 1$

∴ A

Q26

Answer : (D)

Category : Functions

Explanation

그래프에서 $f(x) = 1$이 되는 지점을 찾으면, $(-4, 1)$ 점과 $1 \leq x \leq 3$일 때 $f(x)$값이 1이다.

∴ D

Q27

Answer : (D)

Category : Graphs and Data Analysis

Explanation

그래프를 보면 20~30분 정도까지는 insulated된 container의 rate of temperature change가 non-insulated container보다 더 작은 것을 알 수 있다. 40분이 넘어가는 시점부터는 non-insulated container는 rate of change가 거의 0에 가까워진다.

∴ D

Q28

Answer : (B)

Category : Functions, Coordinate Geometry

Explanation

□ABCD가 square라고 했으므로 diagonal들이 서로 perpendicular하다. 따라서 $\overline{EC} \perp \overline{BD}$이므로 slope of $\overline{EC}$ × slope of $\overline{BD} = -1$

$\rightarrow \dfrac{2-0}{7-1} \times$ slope of $\overline{BD} = -1$

$\rightarrow$ slope of $\overline{BD} = -3$

$\overline{BD}$가 E를 지나므로 $(1, 0)$을 지난다.

따라서 $y - 0 = -3(x - 1)$

∴ B

Q29

Answer : (B)

Category : Equations

Explanation

$y = 3$

$y = ax^2 + b$

Two real solution이 있어야 하므로 $y=3$와 $y=ax^2+b$가 intersection이 2개 있어야 한다. 따라서 경우를 나누어 생각해보면,

(i) $a > 0$ (concave−up)

    $y-$intercept < 3

    $\rightarrow b < 3$

(ii) $a < 0$ (concave−down)

    $y-$intercept > 3

    $\rightarrow b > 3$

$\therefore$ B

Q30

Answer : (A)

Category : Triangles, Polygons

Explanation

Regular hexagon의 넓이 $= 384\sqrt{3}$ in^2

Hexagon을 6개의 regular triangle로 나누어서 생각하면 regular triangle의 넓이

$= \dfrac{384\sqrt{3}}{6} = 64\sqrt{3}$ in^2

각 side가 a인 regular triangle의 넓이

$= \dfrac{\sqrt{3}}{4}a^2 = 64\sqrt{3}$

$\rightarrow a^2 = 256$ in^2

각 side가 a인 square의 넓이 $= a^2 = 256$ in^2

$\therefore$ A

Q31

Answer : 14

Category : Ratio

Explanation

1.5 ft per year라고 했으므로 21 ft가 되려면

$\dfrac{21}{1.5} = 14$ years

$\therefore$ 14

Q32

Answer : 7

Category : Ratio

Explanation

h hours and 30 minutes라고 했고, 1 hour에는 60 minutes가 있으므로 $60h + 30 = 450$

$\rightarrow h = 7$ hours

$\therefore$ 7

Q33

Answer : 11

Category : Functions

Explanation

$f(x) = 3x^2 - bx + 12$ 그래프 위에 $(3, 6)$이 있다고 했으므로

$6 = 3 \times 3^2 - 3b + 12 \rightarrow b = 11$

$\therefore$ 11

Q34

Answer : 105

Category : Equations

Explanation

Doug가 lab에 있었던 시간$= x$

Laura가 lab에 있었던 시간$= y$ 라고 한다면,

$x + y = 250$

$x = y + 40$

$2y + 40 = 250 \rightarrow y = 105, x = 145$

$\therefore$ 105

Q35

Answer : 15

Category : Equations

Explanation

$a = 18t + 15$ 식에서 t가 number of weeks이므로 t의 coefficient인 18이 weekly deposit이다. 따라서 남은 15가 initial deposit인 것이 가장 logical하다.

$\therefore 15$

Q36

Answer : 32

Category : Circles

Explanation

LM과 NM이 tangent라고 했으므로

$\angle MLO = \angle MNO = 90° \rightarrow \angle LON = 120°$

Circumference가 96이므로

$\widehat{LN} = 96 \times \dfrac{120}{360} = 32$

$\therefore 32$

Q37

Answer : 3284

Category : Equations

Explanation

Population을 this year 기준으로 N_0라고 하고 순차적으로 $N_1, N_2, N_3, \cdots$ 라고 한다면,

$K = 4000$

$N_0 = 3000$

$N_1 = N_0 + 0.2(N_0)\left(1 - \dfrac{N_0}{K}\right)$

$\quad = 3000 + 0.2 \times 3000 \times \left(1 - \dfrac{3000}{4000}\right) = 3150$

$N_2 = N_1 + 0.2(N_1)\left(1 - \dfrac{N_1}{K}\right)$

$\quad = 3150 + 0.2 \times 3150 \times \left(1 - \dfrac{3150}{4000}\right) \cong 3284$

$\therefore 3284$

Q38

Answer : 7500

Category : Equations

Explanation

$N_0 = 3000$

$N_1 = N_0 + 0.2(N_0)\left(1 - \dfrac{N_0}{K}\right)$

$\quad = 3000 + 0.2 \times 3000 \times \left(1 - \dfrac{3000}{K}\right)$

$\quad = 3000 + 600\left(1 - \dfrac{3000}{K}\right) = 3360$

$\rightarrow \left(1 - \dfrac{3000}{K}\right) = \dfrac{360}{600} = \dfrac{6}{10}$

$\rightarrow K = 7500$

$\therefore 7500$

Part 3

Practice Test #3

Part III

Practice Test #3

Section 1. Reading Test

Passage I. "The Schartz-Metterklume Method"

Passage Summary

Lines

- **1-8:** A lady is waiting for a train when she sees a loaded cart coming up the road. The man in the cart does not look like a good person because he is treating the horse badly.
- **8-23:** Lady Carlotta tries to help animals usually, even though her friends advise her against it. Except for the time when a boar attacked a friend and Lady Carlotta was working on a painting. She lost the friendship of the lady who was ultimately rescued.
- **24-32:** The train leaves without her because she stops to help the horse, and the Lady sends a telegram to tell her friends she will be late, but her friends are used to her being late for no clear reason.
- **32-48:** As Lady Carlotta tries to figure out what to do next, another lady, Mrs. Quabarl, arrives and thinks that Lady Carlotta is Miss Hope, the governess (home teacher) she has come to meet. Lady Carlotta does not tell her she is wrong.
- **49-61:** As a result Lady Carlotta ends up going with Mrs. Quabarl to her home and learns about her children, who are artistic and delicate.
- **62-75:** Mrs. Quabarl instructs Lady Carlotta on how to teach her children. She wants them not only educated but interested in their studies. She wants them to learn French, and Lady Carlotta says she will teach them French and Russian. The two don't agree.
- **76-end:** Lady Carlotta does not respond as expected to Mrs. Quabarl's posturing and it makes Mrs. Quabarl very uncomfortable.

Main Idea

Lady Carlotta, an unusual lady, pretends to be a governess when Mrs. Quabarl mistakes her for one at the train station. While they are going home together, Mrs. Quabarl tells Lady Carlotta about her expectations, and is taken aback by Lady Carlotta's rebelliousness.

Tone

Highly humorous, tongue-in-cheek, dry

Vocabulary

Line 2	wayside	n. 길가, 도로변
Line 3	uninteresting length	따분한 길이
Line 6	ample	a. 충분한
Line 6	carter	n. 짐마차꾼
Line 7	sullen	a. 뚱한, 시무룩한
Line 9	betook	v. 가다
Line 11	wont	a. ~하는 버릇[습관]이 있는
Line 12	admonition	n. 책망, 경고
Line 12	undesirability	n. 바람직하지 않음, 탐탁지 않음
Line 16	eloquent	a. 웅변[연설]을 잘 하는, 유창한
Line 16	besiege	v. 포위하다, 에워싸다
Line 18	may-tree	n. 산사나무 (hawthorn)
Line 18	boar-pig	n. 수퇘지
Line 21	engaged on	~하느라 바쁜
Line 12	boar	n. 야생돼지, 수퇘지
Line 26	steamed off	(증기선이) 출항했다
Line 27	desertion	n. 내버림, 유기, 방치
Line 30	non-committal	a. 의견[입장]을 밝히지 않는, 어정쩡한
Line 34	imposingly attired	인상적인 복장을 한
Line 35	prolong	v. 연장하다
Line 36	governess	n. 여자 가정교사
Line 37	apparition	n. 유령
Line 40	meekness	n. 온순함, 부드러움
Line 43	alleged	a. ~라고 하는, 소위 ~
Line 46	correctitude	n. (품행의) 방정
Line 49	provoking	a. 짜증나는, 약 오르는
Line 55	thrust	n. 밀치다, 찌르다
Line 58	temperament	n. 기질
Line 59	mould	n. 거푸집, 틀; (사람, 사물의) 타입[유형]
Line 67	commit ~ to memory	~을 마음에 새기다[기억하다]
Line 77	perch	n. 횃대; 높은 자리[위치]
Line 78	self-assured	a. 자신감 있는

Line 78	autocratic	*a.* 독재의, 독재적인
Line 81	render	*v.* ~하게 만들다
Line 82	cowed	*a.* 주눅이 든
Line 82	apologetic	*a.* 미안해하는
Line 85	allude	*v.* 넌지시 말하다
Line 87	discomfiture	*n.* 실패, 당황; 완패
Line 87	patroness	*n.* 여성 후원자
Line 87	abject	*a.* 극도로 비참한, 절망적인
Line 89	warfare	*v.* 전쟁을 치르다
Line 89	behold	*v.* 바라보다
Line 90	battle–elephant	*a.* 전투 코끼리
Line 90	ignominious	*a.* 수치스러운, 창피한
Line 91	slinger	*n.* 투석기
Line 91	javelin	*n.* 투창

Questions

Q1 THING: Main Idea

Answer Key : (B)

Lines 32–35: train station 에서 기차를 기다리고 있던 Lady Carlotta 에게 Mrs. Quabarl 이 다가와서 Lady Carlotta를 "Miss Hope"라 부른다. Lady Carlotta는 이에 대해 "Very well, if I must I must" 라고 반응 → 자신은 Miss Hope가 아닌 Lady Carlotta라고 Mrs. Quabarl을 correct 하지 않는다.

Eliminate

(A), (C), (D) Lady Carlotta는 애초에 Mrs. Quabarl이 고용한 사람이 아니므로, accepting a new job, new employer not mentioned / revenge not mentioned

Q2 THING: Vocabulary

Answer Key : (C)

Lines 1–3: Lady Carlotta는 train에서 station platform에 내린 후, "kill time"하기 위해 "took a turn or two up and down its uninteresting length" 했다고 한다. 이 context에서 "turn"은 short walk를 의미한다.

Eliminate

(A), (B), (D) wrong meaning

Q3 THING: Point of View

Answer Key : (A)

Line 10–14: Lady Carlotta의 acquaintance들은 그녀가 "none of her business"인 일에 interfere한다고 admonish 한다. 즉 Lady Carlotta가 outspoken하다고 생각한다.

Second best answer: (D)

Lines 22-24에서 Lady Carlotta 가 "lost the friendship of the ultimately rescued lady" 한 것으로 보아 그녀가 unfriendly하다고 생각할 수도 있지만, context를 살펴보면 이 사건은 평소 Lady Carlotta의 성격에 반대되는 일이었음

Eliminate

(B), (C), (D) tactful, ambitious, unfriendly한 내용 not mentioned / exception

Q4　THING: Line Evidence

Answer Key : (A)

3번 문제에서 other people이 Lady Carlotta를 어떻게 생각하는지 묻고 있으므로, keyword인 "acquaintances"가 나온 문장을 찾아보자.

Second Best Answer

3번 문제에서 오답인 D를 골랐다면, 이 문제의 답으로 B를 고를 수도 있었을 것이지만, ultimately rescued lady 뿐만이 아닌 "other people"이 Lady Carlotta를 어떻게 생각하는지에 대한 내용은 A에 나와 있음

Eliminate

(B), (C), (D) 다른 사람들이 Lady Carlotta를 어떻게 생각하는지에 대한 내용 not mentioned

Q5　THING: Tone

Answer Key : (C)

Lines 14-22: Lady Carlotta가 interfere하지 않았던 여자는 Lady Carlotta의 "most eloquent exponents" 중 한 명, 즉 Lady Carlotta 가 다른 사람 일에 너무 interfere 한다고 admonish했던 여자이다. 하필 그 여자가 위기에 처했을 때 "put the doctrine of non-interference into practice"한 것은 Lady Carlotta에게 sense of humor가 있다는 점을 보여준다.

Eliminate

(A), (B), (D) Lady Carlotta가 interfere하지 않은 것은 deceptive, cruel, sudden change of behavior 때문이 아닌, 그 여자가 Lady Carlotta에게 했던 말을 humorous하게 적용한 것임

Q6　THING: Vocabulary

Answer Key : (A)

Lines 53-61: narrator는 Mrs. Quabarl이 Lady Carlotta에게 "nature of the charge"를 설명한다고 하고, 그 후에는 Quabarl children이 어떤지 설명하는 내용이 나온다. Context 상 "charge"는 Lady Carlotta의 governess로서의 responsibilities를 의미한다.

Eliminate

(B), (C), (D) wrong meaning

Q7 THING: List

Answer Key : (A)

Lines 53–58: Mrs. Quarbarl은 Claude, Wilfrid, Irene에 대해 설명한 후, Viola에 대해 "something or other else of a mould equally commonplace among children of that class and type"이라고 함 → 모든 Quarbarl children이 그 시대 또래 아이들과 "of a mould equally commonplace"한 skills 를 가지고 있다.

Eliminate

(B), (C), (D) unusually creative and intelligent, hostile to the idea of having a governess, more educated than their peers는 not mentioned

Q8 THING: Quotes, Contrasting Pair

Answer Key : (B)

Lines 62–69: Mrs. Quabarl은 아이들이 "INTERESTED"하기를 바란다고 강조한다. 이를 위해 Lady Carlotta 는 수업을 할 때 아이들이 "committing a mass of historical figures and dates to memory" 하기 보다 는 "feel that they are being introduced to the life-stories"하도록 해야 한다고 함 → 아이들의 active engagement를 원한다.

Eliminate

(A), (C) traditional values, artistic experimentation은 not mentioned

(D) factual retention (= memorizing figures and dates)은 Mrs. Quabarl이 원하는 것의 opposite

Q9 THING: Contrasting Pair

Answer Key : (B)

Lines 77–82: Mrs. Quabarl 의 두 가지 모습에 관한 내용이다. Mrs. Quabarl 은 겉으로는 "magnificent and autocratic"하지만, 누군가 "unexpected resistance"를 보이면 "cowed and apologetic"해진다.

Eliminate

(A), (C), (D) Mrs. Quabarl이 selfish, bitter, frequently imprudent하다는 내용 not mentioned

Q10 THING: Line Evidence

Answer Key : (D)

9번 문제에 대한 답의 keywords인 "magnificent and autocratic", "cowed and apologetic"을 찾아보자.

Eliminate

(A), (B) railway companies와 education에 대한 Mrs. Quabarl의 opinions

(C) Lady Carlotta 에 대한 내용

Passage II. "Saving our Cities from the Automobile"

Passage Summary

Lines
- **1-9:** While there are lots of cars, most of us travel by public transportation.
- **10-19:** Around the globe, public transportation market is growing, and owning a private car is considered unusual.
- **20-34:** However, many people in North America hate public transportation such as buses, subways, and airplanes because the experience is overly negative.
- **35-57:** In contrast, Asian and European cities have developed public transportation so that it is faster and more comfortable than driving your own car.
- **55-81:** The younger generation prefers public transportation because you can use mobile devices more easily on public transportation. More and more of the older generation is also using public transportation because they move to old cities, where you can walk or ride a bike easily.
- **82-85:** We can learn from other countries' public transportation and make ours better.

Main Idea

The automobile industry is growing weaker. We should learn from other countries and upgrade our own public transportation.

Tone

Persuasive, enthusiastic

Vocabulary

Line 4	commuter	n. 통근하는 사람, 통근 ~
Line 7	straphanger	n. (전철 등에서) 손잡이를 잡고 선 사람
Line 18	combustion	n. 연소, 불이 탐
Line 19	anomaly	n. 변칙, 이례
Line 21	glamour	n. (흔히 부와 신분에 따른) 화려함[매력]
Line 21	squalid	a. 지저분한, 불결한
Line 22	impaired	a. 손상된, 제 기능을 못하는
Line 23	decrepit	a. 노후한, 노쇠한
Line 25	transit	n. (대중)교통

Line 28	lurching	n. 갑작스럽게 흔들리는, 비틀거리는
Line 31	underfunded	a. 자금난을 겪는
Line 38	levitation	n. 공중부양
Line 38	skim over	스치듯 날아가다
Line 39	whisk	v. ~을 휙 채어가다, 데려가다
Line 43	cobblestone	n. 자갈, 조약돌
Line 45	seamlessly	ad. 이음매가 없이, 균일하게
Line 45	ramified	a. (작게) 분기된, 나눠진
Line 51	mired	a. 수렁[궁지]에 빠진
Line 52	dawn-to-dusk	a. 새벽부터 황혼까지의
Line 54	stride	n. (성큼성큼 걷는) 걸음
Line 55	sheer	a. 순전한
Line 55	livability	n. 생존율
Line 56	viable	a. 실행 가능한, 성공할 수 있는
Line 58	credit	v. 믿다
Line 58	demographer	n. 인구 통계학자
Line 59	Millenials	n. (Generation Y라고 불리기도 하는) 신세대, 인터넷 세대 (1980~1995년 사이에 출생한 세대)
Line 66	insulation	n. 절연, 방음
Line 67	annoyance	n. 짜증거리, 피곤한 것
Line 71	Leave It to Beaver	전원에서 사는 '완벽한' 가족의 생활상을 다룬 1950년대 미국 TV 드라마
Line 72	contingent	n. 대표단 (여기서는 baby boomer들의 일부)
Line 81	suburban	a. 교외의, 시골의
Line 84	opt	v. ~하기로 택하다

Questions

Q11 THING: Main Idea, Transition Word

Answer Key : (A)

Passage 전체의 main idea는 public transportation이 좋다는 것이다. 하지만 third paragraph는 contrast를 나타내는 transition word인 "And yet" 으로 시작하고, public transportation의 여러 limitation에 대한 내용이다: "depressing experience"(lines 25-26), "underfunded, ill-maintained, and ill-planned"(lines 31).

Eliminate

(B), (C), (D) third paragraph는 전체 passage의 main idea와 contrast하는 내용. Expand upon an argument from first two paragraphs, overview of problem, advocate ending the use of public transportation은 not mentioned

Q12 THING: Point of View, Question

Answer Key : (C)

Line 32-34: "hopping in a car almost always gets you to your destination more quickly" → automobile의 장점은 speed이다.

Eliminate

(A), (B), (D) environmental impact에 대한 내용 not mentioned / convenience, cost는 automobile의 장점으로 directly stated되지 않음

Q13 THING: Line Evidence

Answer Key : (D)

각 answer 의 subject를 잘 살펴보자. 12번 문제의 keyword는 "advantage of automobile travel"이었다. Automobile travel, 다른 말로 "hopping in a car"가 subject가 되는 답은 D이다.

Eliminate

(A), (B), (C) keywords가 not mentioned

Q14 THING: Contrasting Pair, List

Answer Key : (B)

Lines 36-37: narrator는 public transportation이 "faster, more comfortable, and cheaper than the private automobile"이라 주장하고, paragraph 내에서 Shanghai, French towns, Spain to Sweden 등 여러 지역에서 public transportation을 잘 활용한 example들을 list하고 있다.

Second Best Answer : (A), (D)

(A), (D) narrator가 준 example 중 하나의 내용이지만, central idea는 아님

Eliminate

(A), (C), (D) not mentioned / not the central idea

Q15 THING: Line Evidence

Answer Key : (B)

14번에서 paragraph의 central idea를 물었으므로, keyword인 public transportation이 subject인 문장을 찾아야 한다.

Eliminate

(A) keyword인 public transportation이 not mentioned

(C), (D) keywords are not the subject

Q16 THING: Vocabulary

Answer Key : (C)

마지막 paragraph에서 author은 20th century 사람들이 그 전 generation 사람들보다 더 willing to use public transportation이라고 주장한다. 이를 support하는 data로 demographers를 mention한다: "If you credit the demographers, this transit trend has legs" (lines 58–59) → context 상 "credit"은 believe를 뜻한다.

Eliminate

(A), (B), (D) wrong meaning

Q17 THING: Vocabulary

Answer Key : (B)

Lines 59–63: end of 20th century에 adult가 되는 사람들은 cities보다 suburbs를 좋아하고, city에서 쓰이는 public transportation("buses and subways")을 기꺼이 이용한다는 내용 → context 상 "favor"는 prefer를 뜻한다.

Eliminate

(A), (C), (D) wrong meaning

Q18 THING: List

Answer Key : (B)

Lines 63–67: author는 public transportation을 이용하는 사람들이 personal electronic devices를 쓸 수 있다고 하고, 그런 device의 examples를 list한다: "iPads, MP3 players, Kindles, and smartphones"

Eliminate

(A), (C), (D) personal electronic devices에 대한 내용 not mentioned

Q19 THING: Graph

Answer Key : (A)

Figure 1을 보면 10.7%의 public transportation passenger가 students이고 6.7%는 retiree임 → retirees보다 students가 public transportation을 더 많이 이용한다.

Eliminate

(B), (C) Figure 1에 의하면 employed people이 unemployed people이나 homemakers보다 public transportation을 더 많이 이용함

(D) Figure 1만 보고 passengers가 얼마나 frequent하게 public transportation을 이용하는지 알 수 없음

Q20 THING: Graph

Answer Key : (A)

Figure 1에서 72%의 public transportation passengers가 "employed outside home"임을 알 수 있고, Figure 2에서는 59.1%의 public transportation trips가 "work"를 위한 것임을 알 수 있음 → 두 정보를 합치면, 많은 public transportation passengers는 public transportation을 타고 place of employment로 간다는 것을 알 수 있다.

Eliminate

(B), (C), (D) Figure 1과 2에는 passengers use public transportation to run errands, use their own car on weekends, plan to purchase a car에 대한 내용 not mentioned

Passage III. "Feathers"

Passage Summary

Lines

1-11: When he observed the behavior of young birds, Dial wanted to end the old debate about whether birds started to fly by going from trees to ground, or ground to trees.

12-32: He set up a lab to observe, and a rancher told him he needed to provide the birds with something to climb on, which he did.

33-43: The birds used both their wings and their legs to climb up the perches, which gave Dial an idea.

44-59: He recorded the birds running up inclined ramps. As the angle of the ramp increased, they changed the way they held their wings, which were acting as spoilers to manipulate air resistance and help them climb.

60-68: He called this technique WAIR, and discovered it in many different bird species. Some could ascend ramps steeper than 90° degrees.

69-end: WAIR explains a lot about how flight may have evolved.

Main Idea

Dial set up experiments that showed flight may have evolved from ground birds using their wings to help them run up steep inclines.

Tone

Informative, narrative

Vocabulary

Line 2	pheasant	n.	꿩
Line 2	quail	n.	메추라기
Line 2	tinamou	n.	티나무 (중남미의 메추라기 비슷한 새)
Line 5	flap	v.	퍼덕거리다
Line 8	age–old	a.	아주 오래된
Line 9	ground–up–tree–down	a.	"(조류의 진화 방향이) 땅에서 위쪽으로인지 아니면 나무 위에서 내려 온 것인지에 대한" (논쟁)
Line 10	game bird	n.	사냥감 새, 엽조
Line 12	Chukar Partridge	n.	메추라기닭 (닭목 꿩과의 조류)

Line 15	rancher	n. (특히 북미, 오스트레일리아의 대규모) 목장 주인
Line 20	incredulous	a. 믿지 않는, 못 믿겠다는 듯한
Line 27	ledge	n. 절벽에서 (선반처럼) 튀어나온 바위
Line 27	perch	n. (새들이 종종 앉아있는) 횃대
Line 30	hay bale	n. 건초 꾸러미
Line 30	perch on	v. (특히 무엇의 꼭대기나 끝에) 걸터앉다
Line 40	dash out	v. 급히 뛰쳐나가다
Line 45	locomotion	n. 운동, 이동; 여행
Line 46	ingenious	a. (사물, 계획, 생각 등이) 기발한; 독창적인
Line 47	race up	v. (~을) 뛰어 올라가다
Line 47	textured	a. (밋밋하지 않고) 특별한 질감이 나게 만든
Line 47	ramp	n. 경사진 길 또는 계단
Line 47	tilted	a. 기울어진, 경사진
Line 53	spoiler	n. 스포일러 (자동차가 고속으로 달릴 때 차가 들리지 않게 해 주는 부가장치)
Line 54	analogy	n. 비유
Line 56	traction	n. (차량 바퀴의) 정지 마찰력
Line 57	scramble up	v. 기어오르다
Line 70	with one fell swoop	단번에, 한 방에
Line 71	viable	a. 실행 가능한, 성공할 수 있는
Line 73	shortcoming	a. 결점, 단점
Line 75	drawback	n. 결점, 문제점

Questions

Q21 THING: Main Idea

Answer Key : (D)

Sequence of events를 하나 하나 살펴보자.

Event 1: Ken Dial은 evolution of flight을 study하기 위해 baby Chukars가 어떻게 나는 법을 배우는지 observe했다고 한다.

Event 2: Lines 38–43에서 Dial은 Chukars가 unusual하게도 "use their wings and legs cooperatively"한다는 것을 알아챘다. 이것을 더욱 자세히 observe하기 위해 line 46에서 "a series of ingenious experiments"를 만들어 내었다.

Event 3: Lines 49–50에서 Dial은 baby birds가 "angle their wings differently from birds in flight"한다는 것을 알아냈다.

Eliminate

(A), (B), (C) sequence of events가 정확하지 않음

Q22 THING: Vocabulary

Answer Key : (A)

Lines 6–9: Dial의 학생들이 Dial에게 오랫동안 debate되었던 science theory에 대한 new data를 develop해 보라고 "challenge", 즉 dare했다.

Eliminate

(B), (C), (D) wrong meaning

Q23 THING: Problem

Answer Key : (A)

Lines 8–11: Dial이 처음 experiment를 했을 때는 "new data on the age-old ground-up-tree-down debate"를 create하기 위해서 "how baby game birds learned to fly"를 observe하면서 "clues"를 찾으려고 했다. Passage의 맨 처음에 "age-old ground-up-tree-down debate"가 무엇인지 설명되었고, how birds evolved to fly에 대한 이론 두 가지를 제시한다. 마지막으로 passage의 마지막 문단은 WAIR의 evolutionary context를 discuss한다.

Eliminate

(B), (C), (D) Dial의 experiment와 관련 없는 내용 / passage에 의하면 사실이 아님

Q24 THING: Line Evidence

Answer Key : (B)

각 answer choice의 subject를 잘 살펴보자. Keyword인 Dial의 experiment의 assumption이 subject가 되는 문장은 B이다.

Second best answer: (A)

Dial이 baby birds를 관찰했다는 내용이기는 하지만, experiment에 관한 내용 not mentioned

Eliminate

(A), (C), (D) experiment not mentioned/assumption not mentioned

Q25 THING: Main Idea, Quotes

Answer Key : (B)

Dial의 laboratory setup을 본 rancher는 Chukar들이 땅에 있는 것을 보고 "incredulous"해 하면서 새들은 "something to climb on"이 필요하다고 Dial에게 말했다. 이것은 Dial에게 "key piece of advice"(line 14)이였다. Dial은 이 advice 덕분에 나중에 Chukar들이 hay bales에 올라갈 때 다리와 날개를 둘 다 쓰는 것을 볼 수 있었고, 이는 그의 연구의 핵심이 되었다.

Eliminate

(A), (C), (D) second paragraph에서 Dial's motivation for creating the project, differences in laboratory and field research, contributor to a scientific theory는 not mentioned

Q26 THING: Main Idea, Quotes

Answer Key : (C)

Author는 Dial의 "aha moment"가 Chukar들이 "using their wings and legs cooperatively"(lines 40-42)하는 것을 determine했을 때였다고 한다. Dial은 나중에 새들이 gradually steeper inclines를 어떻게 올라가는지 관찰하기 위해 additional experiments를 만들었다: "[he filmed] the birds as they raced up textured ramps tilted at increasing angles"(lines 46-48).

Eliminate

(A), (B), (D)teaching birds to fly, studying videos, consulting other researchers는 not mentioned

Q27 THING: Transition Word

Answer Key : (B)

Lines 49-53: Dial은 Chukar들이 ramp에 올라가면서 "began to flap"하고 "aimed their flapping down and backward, using the force . . . to keep their feet firmly pressed against the ramp"하는 것을 관찰했다. Dial은 이를 통해 position of their flapping wings가 baby Chukar들이 ramp에 올라가는 것을 facilitate했다는 결론을 내렸다.

Eliminate

(A), (C), (D) Chukar's speed, alternation of wing and foot movement, continual hopping motions에 대한 내용 not mentioned

Q28 THING: Vocabulary

Answer Key : (B)

Lines 61-63: Dial은 자신의 연구 결과를 WAIR이라고 이름 붙이고, "went on to document it in a wide range of species"했다고 함 → context 상 "document"는 WAIR이 다양한 새들에게 있음을 record했다는 뜻이다.

Eliminate

(A), (C), (D) wrong meaning

Q29 THING: Contrasting Pair

Answer Key : (D)

Lines 70-74: author는 gliding animal들이 "flapping flight stroke"를 사용하지 않는다고 한다.

Eliminate

(A) gliding animal이 아닌 ground birds에 대한 내용

(B), (C) not mentioned

Q30 THING: Line Evidence

Answer Key : (D)

29번 문제의 키워드인 "gliding animals"가 포함된 lines를 찾아보자.

Eliminate

(A), (B), (C) keyword인 gliding animals에 대한 내용 not mentioned

Passage IV. "Report on Public Instruction" / "A Vindication of the Rights of Woman"

Passage 1

Passage Summary

Lines
- **1-17:** It is hard to explain why women are not allowed to participate in politics. However, excluding women from politics is okay if it makes everyone happy.
- **18-20:** It is best for women that they do not try to change their natural roles.
- **21-30:** Women were not born with the natural qualities necessary for participating in politics. They are too delicate, so they should only do house chores.
- **30-35:** The division of power between men and women in Society is good for harmony. It is proven by the way nature made men and women so different from each other.
- **36-40:** We should respect the other gender and maintain the bond between us since it's for the greater good.

Main Idea

The division of the sexes and keeping women out of politics is better for society and makes everyone happier. It is in everyone's interest to keep the situation of women the same as it is now.

Tone

Persuasive, impassioned, warning

Passage 2

Passage Summary

Lines
- **41-58:** Women should be educated so that they can be good women and do their duties as wives and mothers. But right now, women are not educated and therefore cannot be as good as they should be.

59-71: I challenge Talleyrand's arguments: if the constitution can explain why men should have rights, it should also be able to explain why women can't have them.
72-80: I ask Talleyrand: what right do men have to judge what is best for women's happiness?
81-end: If you do not give women political and civil rights, you are an unreasonable tyrant.

Main Idea

I disagree with Talleyrand; women should be educated and have the same political and civil rights as men.

Tone

Persuasive, impassioned, defiant

Vocabulary

Line 10	institution	n. (특정 집단 사이에서 오랫동안 존재해 온) 제도, 관습
Line 13	exclusion	n. 제외, 배제, 차단
Line 14	decreed	n. 법령, 칙령
Line 17	compel to	강요(강제)해서 ~하게 만들다
Line 17	sanction	v. 허가[승인, 인가]하다
Line 18	reversal	n. (정반대로) 뒤바뀜, 전환, 반전, 역전
Line 21	incontestable	a. 이론[반박]의 여지가 없는
Line 22	aspire	v. 열망[염원]하다
Line 26	constitution	n. 체질; 헌법
Line 26	inclination	n. (~하려는) 의향, 뜻; 성향
Line 28	strenuous	a. 힘이 많이 드는, 몹시 힘든
Line 28	onerous	a. 아주 힘든, 부담되는
Line 35	invoke	v. (법, 규칙 등을) 들먹이다[적용하다]
Line 36	inapplicable	a. 사용[적용]할 수 없는
Line 38	persistence	n. 지속(됨)
Line 41	contend	v. (~을 얻으려고) 다투다[겨루다]
Line 46	inefficacious	a. (약 등이) 효력이 없는
Line 49	virtuous	a. 도덕적인, 고결한
Line 53	patriotism	n. 애국심
Line 58	shut ~ out from …	~을 …에 못 들어가게 하다[차단하다]
Line 59	dispassionately	ad. 냉정하게, 공정하게
Line 66	rest	v. ~을 받치다, 지지하다 (on)

Line 68	parity of	동등한
Line 68	shrink from	~을 꺼리다[피하다], ~에 대해 몸을 사리다
Line 69	prevail	v. 만연[팽배]하다
Line 71	oppression	n. 억압, 탄압; 심한 차별
Line 71	prescription	n. (비유적인 의미에서) 처방[방안]
Line 72	legislator	n. 입법자, 국회의원
Line 75	inconsistent	a. 내용이 다른, 모순되는
Line 76	subjugate	v. 예속시키다, 지배[통제] 하에 두다
Line 79	partake	v. (특히 자기에게 제공된 것을) 먹다[마시다]; 참가하다
Line 80	reason	n. 이성, 사고력
Line 82	denomination	n. 교파, 분파; 여기에서는 '계급'과 비슷한 뜻으로 쓰임
Line 83	crush	n. 으스러뜨리다; 탄압하다
Line 84	assert	v. 주장하다
Line 84	usurp	v. (왕좌, 권좌 등을) 빼앗다[찬탈하다]
Line 87	immure	v. (사람을) 가두다, 유폐시키다
Line 87	groping	a. (깜깜한 곳에서) 손으로 더듬는, 암중모색하는

Questions

Q31 THING: Vocabulary

Answer Key : (B)

Lines 21-24: Passage 1의 authors는 society의 "common happiness, above all that of women"이 여자들이 정치에 involve되지 않아야 이루어질 수 있다고 한다. Society 전체의 happiness를 가리킴 → context 상 "common"은 shared를 뜻한다.

Second best answer: (A)

average는 "평균적인"이라는 뜻으로, "전체적인", "공통된"의 의미로는 쓸 수 없음

Eliminate

(A), (C), (D) wrong meaning in context

Q32 THING: List, Contrasting Pairs

Answer Key : (C)

Lines 26–30에서 authors는 여자들은 본성이 "delicate", "peaceful"하다고 주장한다. 그렇기 때문에 "strenuous habits and onerous duties"가 아닌 "gentle occupations and the cares of the home"에 집중해야 한다고 함 → running a household and raising children은 "strenuous", "onerous"하지 않다는 것을 imply한다.

Eliminate

(A), (B), (D) rewarding for men, less value for society, skills similar to those needed to run a country or a business에 대한 내용 not mentioned

Q33 THING: Line Evidence

Answer Key : (C)

32번 문제의 keywords인 "running a household", "raising children"이 나오는 lines를 찾아보자. Lines 25–30에서 keywords의 synonym인 "cares of the home"이 나온다.

Eliminate

(A), (B), (D) keywords not mentioned

Q34 THING: Main Idea, Problem

Answer Key : (D)

Lines 41–46: Wollstonecraft는 여자들이 "the companion of man"이 되기 위한, 즉 남자들과 비슷한 수준의 education을 받지 않으면 society의 "knowledge and virtue"가 progress하지 않을 것이라고 주장한다.

Eliminate

(A), (B), (C) happiness and financial security, follow societal rules, replace men as figures of power는 not mentioned

Q35 THING: Vocabulary

Answer Key : (C)

Lines 41–46에서 Wollstonecraft는 여자들이 남자들과 비슷한 education을 받아야 truth를 알 수 있을 것이라고 주장한다. 또 education이 "strengthen [women's] reason till she comprehend her duty"(lines 49–50)할 것이라고 주장함 → context 상 "reason"은 intellect를 뜻한다.

Eliminate

(A), (B), (D) wrong meaning

Q36 THING: Contrasting Pair

Answer Key : (A)

Lines 72–78: Wollstonecraft는 society's leaders가 pass한 laws는 남자들이 "contend for their freedom"할 수 있도록 해 주지만, 동시에 "subjugate women"한다고 주장한다. 즉 "subjugate"는 control한다는 뜻이다. Wollstonecraft는 society's leader들이 남자에게는 자유를 보장하면서 여자들에게는 똑같은 자유를 주지 않는다고 생각한다.

Second Best Answer : (C)

Line 77–78에서 happiness를 promote하려던 의도를 mention하지만, arguments를 cause했다는 내용 not mentioned

Eliminate

(B), (C), (D) reduction in individual virtue, arguments about happiness, equality for all people은 not mentioned

Q37 THING: Line Evidence

Answer Key : (D)

36번 문제의 keywords인 "freedom", "society's leaders"가 나온 lines를 찾아보자. Lines 72–75에 context상 "society's leaders"의 synonym인 "legislator"와 "freedom"이 나온다.

Eliminate

(A), (B), (C) keywords가 나오지 않음

Q38 THING: Point of View, Quotes

Answer Key : (C)

Wollstonecraft가 quote한 passage 1의 statement: political participation에서 여자를 exclude하는 것은 "according to abstract principles . . . impossible to explain"(lines 61–65). 그 다음에 Wollstonecraft는 passage 1의 authors가 "the abstract rights of man"을 discuss할 수 있다면, 여자들의 abstract rights도 discuss할 수 있어야 한다고 주장함(lines 66–69) → Wollstonecraft는 passage 1의 authors가 present한 reasonings의 flaw를 highlight하면서 자신의 argument를 develop하고 있다.

Eliminate

(A), (B), (D) authors' qualifications, women excluded by their own government (passage 1의 첫번째 문장), authors' conclusions on gender roles에 대한 내용 not mentioned

Q39 THING: Main Idea, Point of View, Contrasting Pairs

Answer Key : (A)

Passage 1의 main idea는 여자의 자유를 restrict하는 것이 "impossible to explain"(line 7)하지만, society's overall happiness를 위해 필요(lines 13–17)하다고 주장한다. Passage 2는 이러한 주장을 strongly challenge한다: "Who made man the exclusive judge [of which freedoms are granted to women]?"(line 78–80)라고 묻는다; 여자의 "civil and political rights"를 억압하는 society's male leaders를 tyrants에 비교한다(lines 81–88).

Eliminate

(B), (C), (D) passage 1과 passage 2의 관계를 정확히 나타내지 못함

Q40 THING: Point of View

Answer Key : (D)

Passage 1의 authors는 여자들이 "excluded by the other half [men] from any participation in government"(lines 1–2)라고 인정하고, Wollstonecraft는 society's male leaders들이 만든 laws는 여자들의 "civil and political rights"(line 86)를 restrict한다고 주장함 → 두 passage의 authors 모두 여자들이 남자들보다 누리는 rights가 적다고 한다.

Eliminate

(A), (B) passage 1의 authors는 여자와 남자의 natural preference가 정반대라고 주장(lines 25–30) / women's education이나 success에 대한 내용 not mentioned

(C) Wollstonecraft는 여자들이 happy하다고 생각하지 않고 오히려 "groping in the dark"한다고 생각함 (lines 85–88)

Q41 THING: Point of View, Contrasting Pairs

Answer Key : (A)

Passage 2 마지막 paragraph에서 Wollstonecraft는 society's male leaders가 "tyrants"처럼 여자들의 "civil and political rights"를 억압한다고 주장한다(lines 81–88). Passage 1에 의하면 society's leaders는 "wishes of nature"(line 25)에 따라 법을 만들어야 하는데, nature가 여자와 남자를 다르게 만들었으므로 여자와 남자에게 똑같은 rights 와 roles 를 줄 수 없다고 주장함 (lines 30–36). Passage 1의 authors는 여자들에게 이러한 rights를 주는 것은 "a reversal of [society's] primary destinies"(lines 18–19)라고 주장할 것이다.

Eliminate

(B), (C), (D) passage 1의 authors들의 주장과 반대

Passage V. "Honey Bee Colony Collapse Disorder is ..."

Passage Summary

Lines

1-7: Varroa mites live on honey bees and kill them directly or cause additional harm by weakening them. Yet, it is unknown how bees naturally keep mites under control.

7-18: Plants called pyrethrums produce chemicals that stop mite activity.

19-30: Commercial bees that don't feed on pyrethrums probably do not have the nutrients that will protect them from the mites.

31-41: Man–made insecticides can be more dangerous because the wrong amount of such chemicals can be poisonous to the bees. So we think it is better to let the bees control the amount for themselves, by planting different flowers that contain pyrethrum around the bee hive.

42-50: One can test this by giving Pyrethrum plants to one group of bees and regular clovers to another group of bees. By counting the number of bees affected by mites, one can see the difference between the two groups.

51-end: By testing with wild bees, one can also see the difference between the bees' choice of plants.

Main Idea

Bees that don't feed on pyrethrum–containing plants are probably likely to be infected by Varroa mites. There is an experiment we can do to prove this theory true.

Tone

Informative, speculative, scientifically neutral

Vocabulary

Line 1	pathogenic	*a.* 발병시키는, 병원성의
Line 2	ectoparasitic	*a.* 외부 기생충의
Line 3	hemolymph	*n.* 헤림프 (무척추 동물의 체강과 조직에 흐르는 액체; 절지동물에서는 혈액으로 작용함)
Line 4	susceptibility	*n.* 민감성
Line 8	pyrethrum	*n.* 제충국 꽃 (냉혈동물 중에서도 특히 곤충에 대해 독성이 강한 pyrethrin을 함유하고 있음)

Line 11	potent	n. 강력한
Line 12	insecticide	n. 살충제
Line 15	pyrethrin	n. 피레드린 (제충국의 살충 성분)
Line 16	analogue	n. 유사체
Line 16	pyrethroid	n. 피레드로이드 (피레드린과 비슷한 합성 살충제)
Line 17	infestation	n. 침략; (기생충 등의) 체내 침입
Line 17	scabies	n. 옴, 개선충
Line 18	topical	a. (사람 몸의) 국부, 국소의
Line 20	mono-crop	n. 단일 작물
Line 21	postulate	v. (이론 등의 근거로 삼기 위해 무엇이 사실이라고) 상정하다
Line 24	intermittent	a. 간헐적인, 간간이 일어나는
Line 28	immunocompromised	a. 면역 시스템이 손상[약화]된, 면역 무방비(상태)의
Line 29	viral	a. 바이러스성의
Line 30	fungal	a. 균류[곰팡이]에 의한
Line 30	pathogen	n. 병원균, 병원체
Line 37	left to	~에 맡겨진
Line 39	parasite	n. 기생충

Questions

Q42 THING: Tone

Answer Key : (C)

Passage 전체의 tone을 살펴보자. Authors는 bee colonies의 problems를 discuss할 때 "we suspect"(line 9), "we postulate"(line 21) 등의 phrase를 쓴다. 이는 authors가 hypothesize하고 있다는 것을 보여준다. "can", "may", "could"는 모두 "~할 수도 있다"는 의미로, 역시나 tentative tone을 create하는 데 도움을 준다.

Second Best Answer

Authors들이 confidence가 없는 것은 사실이지만, research의 usefulness에 대해 dubious한 것은 아님

Eliminate

(A), (B), (D) passage 전체의 tone은 optimistic, dubious, critical하지 않음

Q43 THING: Main Idea

Answer Key : (C)

Lines 24-28: authors는 bee colonies가 pyrethrum producing plants를 가끔 먹지 않으면 mite infestations에 걸릴 수 있다고 hypothesize한다. Lines 42-46: 이러한 hypothesis를 test하기 위해 "a small number of commercial honey bee colonies"에게 "a number of pyrethrum producing plants"를 주는 trial을 만들자고 suggest한다.

Eliminate

(A), (D) secondary infection, humans more susceptible to varroa mites에 대한 내용 not mentioned
(B) lines 31-35에 의하면 insecticides는 오히려 bee colonies에게 harmful

Q44 THING: Line Evidence

Answer Key : (D)

43번 문제의 keyword인 "hypothesis"와 "pyrethrum producing plants"가 나오는 lines를 찾아보자. Lines 23-28에서 "can become susceptible"이라고 하는 phrase는 authors가 hypothesize하고 있음을 나타낸다.

Second best answer: (C)

"We suspect"라는 phrase에서도 역시 hypothesis가 imply되지만, 다른 keyword인 "pyrethrum producing plants"가 나오지 않음

Eliminate

(A), (B), (C) keywords가 not mentioned

Q45 THING: Contrasting Pair

Answer Key : (D)

Lines 31-35: beekeepers가 commercially produced insecticides를 써서 mite infections를 해결하려고 하면, "immunocompromised or nutritionally deficient"한 bees를 "further weaken"할 수 있다고 한다.

Eliminate

(A), (B), (C) increase mite population, beneficial bacteria, bees' primary food source 는 not mentioned

Q46 THING: Line Evidence

Answer Key : (C)

45번 문제의 keyword인 "mite infestations"와 "commercially produced insecticides"가 나오는 lines를 찾아보자.

Eliminate

(A), (B), (D) keywords가 not mentioned

Q47　THING: Vocabulary

Answer Key : (B)

　　Lines 31–35: authors는 beekeepers가 commercially produced insecticides를 쓰면 "bees may be further weakened"라고 한다. 그 다음에 mite infestation을 prevent하는 데 필요한 necessary dosage는 bees가 결정하는 것이 낫다고 "we further postulate"이라고 말함 → context 상 "postulate"은 put forth the idea를 뜻한다.

Second best answer: (D)

　　Authors가 conclude했다고 생각할 수도 있지만, 이전 문장에서 "may be"라고 말한 것으로 보아 firm evidence는 아님

Eliminate

　　(A), (C), (D) wrong meaning in context

Q48　THING: Main Idea

Answer Key : (B)

　　4번째 paragraph에서 authors는 honeybees가 pyrethrum producing plants를 먹는 것이 mite infestation을 막는 데 도움이 되는지 연구하기 위한 trial을 propose한다. Experiment에서 authors는 honey bee colonies에게 pyrethrum producing plants와 "a typical bee food source such as clover"을 offer해, 두 가지 다른 diets가 mite infestation에 영향을 주는지 보려고 한다.

Eliminate

　　(A), (D) 이미 실행한 experiment나 unfinished experiment의 결과가 아닌, 앞으로 해 보아야 할 experiment에 대한 내용

　　(C) nutritional analysis는 not mentioned

Q49　THING: Contrasting Pair

Answer Key : (A)

　　Lines 43–45: authors는 "pyrethrum producing plants와 "typical bee food source"인 clover를 contrast하고 있음 → clover는 pyrethrum을 produce하지 않는다고 imply한다.

Second best answer: (B)

　　사실이기는 하지만, passage에서 directly state되었고 imply되지 않았음

Eliminate

　　(B) imply 아님

　　(C), (D) location, good food source에 대한 내용 not mentioned

Q50 THING: Graph

Answer Key : (B)

Table을 보면, colony collapse disorder가 있는 honeybee colonies의 77%가 pathogen 4개 모두에 감염되었다.

Eliminate

(A), (C), (D) table의 내용과 일치하지 않음

Q51 THING: Graph

Answer Key : (D)

Table을 보면, colony collapse disorder가 없는 colony의 81%는 Nosema ceranae pathogen에 감염되었다.

Eliminate

(A), (B), (C) table의 내용과 일치하지 않음

Q52 THING: Graph

Answer Key : (D)

Table은 honeybee colonies 내의 pathogen occurrence를 discuss하지만, mites에 감염되었는지에 대한 내용은 없다. 그러므로 mites가 honeybees의 "susceptibility to secondary infection with fungi, bacteria, or viruses"(lines 4–5)를 증가시켰는지 알 수 없다.

Eliminate

(A), (B) table에는 mite infestation에 대한 내용이 없으므로 알 수 없음

(C) 문제와 관련 없는 이유를 제시하고 있음

Section 2. Writing and Language Test

Q1
Answer : (A)
Category : Parallelism
Explanation
"happier", "healthier", "more productive"는 parallel해야 한다. 정답은 (A)
Eliminate
(B), (C), (D) "healthy", "they are productive", "being more productive"는 "happier"와 parallel하지 않음

Q2
Answer : (B)
Category : Insert/Delete/Replace
Explanation
Passage가 "natural light"의 importance에 대해 이야기하고 있으므로 그 주제를 introduce하는 문장이 가장 적당하다. 정답은 (B)
Eliminate
(A), (C), (D) "light"와 관련이 없음

Q3
Answer : (C)
Category : Insert/Delete/Replace
Explanation
"circadian rhythms"와 관련이 없는 문장은 넣을 수 없다. 정답은 (C)
Eliminate
(A), (B), (D) passage의 흐름을 방해함

Q4
Answer : (C)
Category : Apostrophes
Explanation
General한 "body"의 "biological clocks"이므로 "body"에 apostrophe를 붙여야 한다. 정답은 (C)
Eliminate
(A), (B), (D) "bodies"는 plural / "clock"은 아무 것도 possess할 수 없기 때문에 apostrophe를 쓸 수 없음

Q5
Answer : (A)
Category : Subject-Verb Disagreement - Basic, Wordiness
Explanation
Subject가 singular noun인 "absenteeism"이므로 singular 형태인 "is"를 써야 한다. 정답은 (A)
Eliminate
(B), (D) "are"와 "have been"은 plural form이므로 SVD 오류
(C) "is being"은 wordy

Q6
Answer : (B)
Category : Insert/Delete/Replace
Explanation
앞 문장에서 이야기하고 있는 "productivity"와 관련이 있는 statement가 와야 한다. 정답은 (B)
Eliminate
(A), (C), (D) "productivity"와 관련이 없음

Q7

Answer : (A)
Category : Insert/Delete/Replace
Explanation
　이 문장은 artificial light가 또한 costly하다는 내용을 설명한 paragraph를 introduce한다. 앞에서 나온 "lowering worker productivity"의 내용과, 이 paragraph의 내용을 가장 잘 transition하는 문장은 (A)이다.
Eliminate
　(B) 문장의 verb인 "constitutes"의 subject는 "cost of artificial light sources"가 아닌 "artifical light sources"가 되어야 함
　(C), (D) "lowering worker productivity"의 내용에서 "costly"의 내용으로 transition하지 않음

Q8

Answer : (D)
Category : Redundancy
Explanation
　"annual"과 "each year"는 redundant하므로 하나만 써야 한다. 정답은 (D)
Eliminate
　(A), (B), (C) "annual"과 "each year", "every year", "per year"는 redundant

Q9

Answer : (C)
Category : Vocabulary
Explanation
　"full-pane windows" 대신에 다른 방법인 "light tubes"를 사용할 수 있다는 뜻이므로 다른 대안을 제시하는 conjunctive adverb를 써야 한다. 정답은 (C)
Eliminate
　(A), (B), (D) 대안을 제시하는 conjuctive adverb가 아님

Q10

Answer : (C)
Category : Relative Pronoun
Explanation
　Object인 "light tubes"를 설명하는 subordinating clause를 연결해 주므로 relative pronoun "which"를 써야 한다. 정답은 (C)
Eliminate
　(A), (B), (D) relative pronoun이 아님

Q11

Answer : (B)
Category : Idioms
Explanation
　"a means of"가 correct idiomatic expression이다. 정답은 (B)
Eliminate
　(A), (C), (D) correct idiomatic expression이 아님

Q12

Answer : (A)
Category : Pronoun Shift
Explanation
　Object pronoun이 subject인 "settlers"이므로 plural reflexive pronoun인 "themselves"를 써야 한다. 정답은 (A)
Eliminate
　(B), (D) singular pronouns
　(C) possessive pronoun

Q13

Answer : (C)
Category : Insert/Delete/Replace
Explanation
　앞 문장인 "food [...] of terrible quality"를 해결하는 내용을 introduce하는 문장이어야 한다. 정답은 (C)

Eliminate

(A), (B) "food"와 관련이 없음

(D) 이어지는 문장의 purpose를 설명하지 않음

Q14

Answer : (D)

Category : Period, Semi-colon vs. Comma

Explanation

문장의 verb가 없기 때문에 comma를 넣어서 modifying clause인 "an English-born entrepreneur"를 마무리 짓고 subject인 "Fred Harvey"의 verb phrase를 만들어야 한다. 정답은 (D)

Eliminate

(A), (B), (D) verb 가 없으므로 sentence fragments

Q15

Answer : (B)

Category : SVD - Basic, Pronoun Shift

Explanation

문장의 subject인 "Harvey Houses"는 plural이므로 verb도 plural이고 possessive pronoun도 3$_{rd}$ person plural이어야 한다. 정답은 (B)

Eliminate

(A), (C) singular verb

(D) singular impersonal possessive pronoun

Q16

Answer : (C)

Category : Vocabulary

Explanation

이전의 "food"를 describe하는 "terrbile quality"와 가장 비슷한 "아주 나쁜, 최악"이라는 뜻의 단어를 써야 한다. 정답은 (C)

Eliminate

(A) sinister의 뜻은 "사악한, 해로운"

(B) surly의 뜻은 "무례한"

(D) icky의 뜻은 "기분 나쁜"

Q17

Answer : (C)

Category : Insert/Delete/Replace

Explanation

앞 문장이 "conventional business practices"와 다른 것을 시도했다는 것을 imply하고 뒷 문장이 "advertisement seeking [...] women"에 대한 이야기를 하므로 중간에 "employing women"이 imply했던 시도라는 것을 써야 한다. 정답은 (C)

Eliminate

(A), (B) passage와 흐름에 필요한 문장이므로 delete할 수 없음

(D) specific example은 뒷 문장임

Q18

Answer : (B)

Category : Redundancy

Explanation

"overwhelming"과 "tremendous"는 redundant 하기 때문에 둘 중에 하나만 써야 한다. 정답은 (B)

Eliminate

(A), (C), (D) "overwhelming"과 "tremendous"는 redundant

Q19

Answer : (D)

Category : Incomplete Sentences

Explanation

[Not only...but also...]는 parallel을 이루는 idiomatic expression이다. "not only" clause에 subject와 verb가 있으므로 "but also" clause에도 subject와 verb가 있어야 한다. 정답은 (D)

Eliminate

(A), (B), (C) subject가 없으므로 correct idiomatic expression이 아님

Q20

Answer : (C)

Category : Insert/Delete/Replace

Explanation

"Harvey girls"에 대한 paragraph이므로 앞 문장에 list된 benefits와 "Harvey girls"에 관련되어 있는 문장이어야 한다. 정답은 (C)

Eliminate

(A), (B), (D) paragraph와 관련 없음

Q21

Answer : (D)

Category : Front Modifier

Explanation

"Living independently [...] ethic"은 "Harvey Girls"를 modify하는 front modifier이므로 comma로 끝나야 하고 "Harvey Girls"는 comma 뒤에 가장 처음으로 와야 한다. 정답은 (D)

Eliminate

(A), (B) front modifer이 comma로 끝나지 않음

(C) "Harbey girls"가 comma뒤에 바로 오지 않음

Q22

Answer : (A)

Category : Insert/Delete/Replace

Explanation

"transformative"의 뜻이 "변화시키는"이기 때문에 어떻게 "American West"를 변화시켰는지 examples를 provide하는 문장이 있어야 한다. 정답은 (A)

Eliminate

(B) transition이 아닌 previous sentence를 clarify하기 위한 examples

(C), (D) previous sentence를 clarify하기 위해 필요함

Q23

Answer : (A)

Category : Insert/Delete/Replace, Wordiness

Explanation

"I-MCP"의 effect에 focus하는 문장이 필요하다. 정답은 (A)

Eliminate

(B), (D) "producers"가 subject가 되어 I-MCP에 focus하지 않음

(C) wordy

Q24

Answer : (D)

Category : Back Modifier

Explanation

"a chemical [...] rot"는 ethylene을 modify하는 additional information이기 때문에 subject와 verb는 필요 없다. 정답은 (D)

Eliminate

(A), (B), (C) subject와 verb는 필요 없음

Q25

Answer : (B)

Category : Vocabulary

Explanation

"단단한" 같은 fruit texture를 describe하는 단어가 필요하다. 정답은 (B)

Eliminate

(A) "tight"의 뜻은 "꽉 조여있는"

(C) "stiff"의 뜻은 "뻣뻣한"

(D) "taut"의 뜻은 "팽팽한"

Q26

Answer : (A)
Category : Pronoun Shift, Diction
Explanation
　Possessive pronoun의 antecedent는 "apples"이므로 plural possessive pronoun인 "their"가 필요하다. 정답은 (A)
Eliminate
　(B), (D) possessive pronoun이 아님
　(C) singular possessive pronoun

Q27

Answer : (D)
Category : Relative Pronouns
Explanation
　Person인 "consumers"를 modify하는 subordinating clause를 연결해주므로 relative pronoun "who"를 써야 한다. 정답은 (D)
Eliminate
　(A) "that"은 thing이 antecedent인 경우에 사용
　(B) "they"는 subjective pronoun
　(C) "which"는 thing이 antecedent인 경우에 사용

Q28

Answer : (B)
Category : Tense Form
Explanation
　같은 문장에 present tense인 "do"가 있기 때문에 다른 verb 또한 present tense를 써야 한다. 정답은 (B)
Eliminate
　(A), (C), (D) past tense가 아님

Q29

Answer : (B)
Category : Colons and Dashes
Explanation
　앞 문장과 뒷 문장이 모두 complete sentence이기 때문에 "Bartlett pears"를 설명하는 문장을 introduce하는 colon이 필요하다. 정답은 (B)
Eliminate
　(A), (C), (D) 잘못된 transition

Q30

Answer : (B)
Category : Insert/Delete/Replace
Explanation
　"But"으로 시작하는 sentence이기 때문에 앞 문장의 내용을 contradict하는 내용이 뒷 문장에 나와야 한다. 정답은 (B)
Eliminate
　(A), (C), (D) passage 흐름에 맞지 않음

Q31

Answer : (D)
Category : Graph
Explanation
　그래프의 내용을 가장 잘 나타낸 것은 (D)이다.
Eliminate
　(A) 5%보다 훨씬 많이 줄어든다.
　(B), (C)는 not supported by graph

Q32

Answer : (B)

Category : Graph

Explanation

I-MCP를 받은 사과들은 graph에서 browning에 큰 차이를 보이지 않는다. 바로 controlled atmosphere에 넣은 사과도 50% 조금 안 되게 brown하고, open air부터 놓은 사과들도 50%를 조금 넘게 brown한다. 즉, 둘 다 반쯤 brown 된다. 정답은 (B)

Eliminate

(A), (C), (D) not supported by graph

Q33

Answer : (C)

Category : Insert/Delete/Replace

Explanation

"people in the fruit industry"에 속하는 "fruit sellers"와 "sellers"의 "actions"에 대해 이야기해야 한다. 정답은 (C)

Eliminate

(A), (B), (D) "people in the fruit industry"와 관련 없음

Q34

Answer : (D)

Category : Various Comma Usages

Explanation

"From [...] Gothic"은 subject와 verb가 없는 additional information이자 sentence fragment이기 때문에 뒤에 comma를 넣어서 main clause와 연결해주어야 한다. 정답은 (D)

Eliminate

(A), (B), (C) sentence fragment를 만듦

Q35

Answer : (B)

Category : Colons and Dashes

Explanation

"image of dogs playing poker"를 설명하는 additional information이 dash로 시작됐기 때문에 dash로 끝나야 한다. 정답은 (B)

Eliminate

(A), (C), (D) dash 사용 안 함

Q36

Answer : (C)

Category : SVD

Explanation

문장의 subject가 "works of art"이므로 plural form verb인 "portray"가 나와야 한다. 정답은 (C)

Eliminate

(A), (D) singular verb

(B) gerund가 오면 verb가 없으므로 sentence fragment

Q37

Answer : (D)

Category : Insert/Delete/Replace

Explanation

"Russia"의 "State Hermitage Museum in St. Petersburg"에 대한 이야기를 다루는 다음 passage를 introduce하는 문장이 필요하다. 정답은 (D)

Eliminate

(A), (B), (C) 다음 passage 이야기와 관련 없음

Q38

Answer : (C)

Category : Parallelism

Explanation

Subject가 같은 "could damage"와 parallel한 "(could) scare"가 나와야 한다. 정답은 (C)

Eliminate

(A), (B), (D) "could damage"와 parallel하지 않음

Q39

Answer : (C)

Category : Insert/Delete/Replace

Explanation

"Peter's daughter Elizaveta"에 관한 문장이기 때문에 "Peter the Great"이 나오는 문장 뒤에 나와야 한다. 정답은 (C)

Eliminate

(A), (B), (D) passage에 흐름을 방해함

Q40

Answer : (B)

Category : Vocabulary

Explanation

"paintings"를 "의뢰, 주문하다"는 뜻의 단어가 나와야 한다. 정답은 (B)

Eliminate

(A) "decreed"의 뜻은 "법령을 발표하다"

(C) "forced"의 뜻은 "강요하다"

(D) "licensed"의 뜻은 "허가하다"

Q41

Answer : (D)

Category : Various Comma Usages

Explanation

"digital artist Eldar Zakirov"가 "painted"의 subject인 "person chosen for this task"의 additional information이기 때문에 앞과 뒤에 comma를 넣어야 한다. 정답은 (D)

Eliminate

(A) "Eldar Zairov"는 "painted"의 subject가 아님

(B) "digital artist"뒤에 comma는 필요 없음

(C) "digital" 앞에 comma 필요

Q42

Answer : (A)

Category : Insert/Delete/Replace

Explanation

다음 문장의 "portrait"을 "aristocratic"과 "royal"이 modify하기 때문에 비슷한 뜻의 elevated된 tone의 문장이 와야 한다. 정답은 (A)

Eliminate

(B) "unique chracteristics of each cat"에 관한 이야기 없음

(C) "absurdity"는 disparage하는 tone

(D) "talented mouse catcher"는 passage와 관련 없음

Q43

Answer : (D)

Category : Insert/Delete/Replace

Explanation

"cat"의 "portrait"에 관한 passage이기 때문에 "museum"에 관한 설명은 필요 없다. 정답은 (D)

Eliminate

(A), (B) passage와 관련 없음

(C) "Winter Palace"에 관한 passage가 아님

Q44

Answer : (D)

Category : Insert/Delete/Replace

Explanation

"cats"가 왜 "benefactors of the museum"인지 설명하는 내용이어야 한다. 정답은 (D)

Eliminate

(A), (B), (C) "museum"에 beneficial한 이유를 설명하지 않음

Section 3. Math Test
(No Calculator)

Q1
Answer : (C)
Category : Equations
Explanation

Fee＝$nKlh$에서
$n=$number of walls
$K=$dollars per square foot
$l=$length
$h=$height 라고 했는데 paint의 brand가 바뀌면 결국 cost가 늘어나게 된다. 따라서 wall과 관련된 variable들은 영향을 받지 않고 cost가 더 추가되므로 K가 영향을 받는다.
∴ C

Q2
Answer : (D)
Category : Equations
Explanation

$3r=18$ → $r=6$
$6r+3=39$
∴ D

Q3
Answer : (D)
Category : Powers and Roots
Explanation

$a^{\frac{p}{q}}=\sqrt[q]{a^p}$이므로
$a^{\frac{2}{3}}=\sqrt[3]{a^2}$)
∴ D

Q4
Answer : (B)
Category : Equations
Explanation

1776－1849 사이에 join한 state의 수가
1850－1900 사이에 join한 state 수의 TWICE라고 했으므로 $30=2x$
∴ B

Q5
Answer : (C)
Category : Equations
Explanation

$\frac{5}{x}=\frac{15}{x+20}$ → $15x=5(x+20)=5x+100$
$x=10$
$\frac{x}{5}=\frac{10}{5}=2$
∴ C

Q6
Answer : (C)
Category : Equations
Explanation

$2x-3y=-14$ ······ ①
$3x-2y=-6$ ······ ②
①×2－②×3를 하면
$x=2$, $y=6$
$x-y=-4$
∴ C

Q7

Answer : (C)

Category : Functions

Explanation

Polynomial function의 factor가 되려면 $x-$intercept, 즉 $f(x)=0$이 되어야 한다.
따라서 $f(4)=0$이므로 $x-4$가 $f(x)$의 factor이다.
∴ C

Q8

Answer : (A)

Category : Equations, Functions

Explanation

$y=kx+4$ 그래프 위에 (c, d)가 존재하므로
$d=ck+4 \rightarrow k=\dfrac{d-4}{c}$
그래프의 slope $=k$
∴ A

Q9

Answer : (A)

Category : Equations, Functions

Explanation

$kx-3y=4$
$4x-5y=7$
이 두 그래프가 no solution이기 위해서는 두 그래프의 slope가 같고 $y-$intercept가 달라야 한다.
(intersection이 존재하지 않게)
slope가 같아야 하므로
$\dfrac{k}{-3}=\dfrac{4}{-5} \rightarrow k=\dfrac{12}{5}$
∴ A

Q10

Answer : (A)

Category : Functions, Coordinate Geometry

Explanation

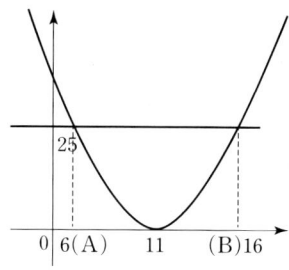

그래프에서 보이듯이 $y=(x-11)^2$의 중앙까지 A와 B가 symmetric하다.
AB$=10$
∴ A

Q11

Answer : (B)

Category : Polygons

Explanation

Opposite Angles의 성질을 이용하면,
$x=t, y=u, z=w$
$x+y=u+t$인데 문제 조건에서
$x+y=u+w$이라고 했으므로
$t=w$
따라서 $x=t=w=z$
∴ B

Q12

Answer : (A)

Category : Functions

Explanation

$y=a(x-2)(x+4)$
$=a(x^2+2x-8)$
$=a(x+1)^2-9a$
$\rightarrow$ Vertex $=(-1, -9a)=(c, d)$
$d=-9a$
∴ A

Q13

Answer : (B)

Category : Equations

Explanation

$$\frac{24x^2+25x-47}{ax-2}=-8x-3-\frac{53}{ax-2}$$
$$=\frac{-(8x+3)(ax-2)-53}{ax-2}$$
$$=\frac{-8ax^2-(3a-16)x-47}{ax-2}$$

True for all values of $x\neq \frac{2}{a}$ 라고 했으므로

$-8a=24 \rightarrow a=-3$

∴ B

Q14

Answer : (A)

Category : Equations

Explanation

$3x^2+12x+6=0 \rightarrow x^2+4x+2=0$

Quadratic Formula를 적용하면

$x=\frac{-4\pm\sqrt{(16-8)}}{2}=-2\pm\sqrt{2}$

∴ A

Q15

Answer : (D)

Category : Ratio, Equations

Explanation

$C=\frac{5}{9}(F-32)=\frac{5}{9}F-\frac{160}{9}$

$F-32=\frac{9}{5}C \rightarrow F=\frac{9}{5}C+32$

I과 II에 있는 1 degree increase를 각 F와 C에 관해 정리한 식에 적용하면 각각 $\frac{5}{9}$와 1.8의 slope를 갖고 있으므로 성립한다.

III에 있는 $\frac{5}{9}$ degree increase를 적용하면

1 degree의 increase가 있지 않기 때문에 성립하지 않는다.

∴ D

Q16

Answer : 1 or 2

Category : Factoring, Equations

Explanation

$x^3(x^2-5)=-4x \rightarrow x^5-5x^3+4x=0$

$x(x^4-5x^2+4)=0$
$=x(x^2-1)(x^2-4)$
$=x(x+1)(x-1)(x-2)(x+2)=0$

$x=0, \pm 1, \pm 2$

$x>0$이므로

$x=1, 2$

∴ 1 or 2

Q17

Answer : 2

Category : Fractions, Equations

Explanation

$\frac{7}{9}x-\frac{4}{9}x=\frac{1}{4}+\frac{5}{12} \rightarrow \frac{1}{3}x=\frac{8}{12}=\frac{2}{3}$

$x=2$

∴ 2

Q18

Answer : 105

Category : Polygons

Explanation

$180-z=2y, \; y=75$

$\rightarrow z=30$

$x=180-\frac{180-30}{2}=105°$

∴ 105

Q19

Answer : 370

Category : Equations

Explanation

Hamburger의 calories $= x$

Fries의 calories $= y$ 라고 했을 때,

$x = y + 50$

$2x + 3y = 1700$

$\rightarrow 2(y+50) + 3y = 1700$

$y = 320, \ x = 370$

$\therefore 370$

Q20

Answer : $\frac{3}{5}$ or .6

Category : Triangles, Trigonometry

Explanation

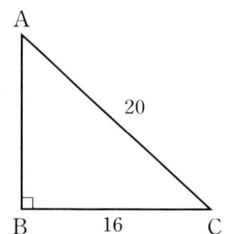

문제에 주어진 대로 도형을 그려보면 위와 같다.

$\overline{AB} = \sqrt{\overline{AC}^2 - \overline{BC}^2} = \sqrt{20^2 - 16^2} = 12$

$\triangle ABC \sim \triangle DEF$이고 similarity ratio는 $\frac{1}{3}$이라고 했으므로

$\sin F = \dfrac{\frac{12}{2}}{\frac{20}{3}} = \dfrac{3}{5}$

$\therefore \dfrac{3}{5}$ or .6

Section 4. Math Test
(Calculator)

Q1
Answer : (C)
Category : Graphs and Data Analysis
Explanation

30분 동안 lunch를 먹었다고 했으므로 그 동안은 distance의 변화가 없다. 따라서 distance 변화가 없는 구간을 찾으면 1:00 PM–2:00 PM 이다. Hiking을 continue한 시점을 찾아야 하므로 2:00 PM에 가까운 시간대를 찾으면 된다.
∴ C

Q2
Answer : (B)
Category : Probability,
             Graphs and Data Analysis
Explanation

Either a female under age 40 OR a male age 40 or older 라고 했으므로 두 probability를 더하면 된다.
따라서 Probability $= \frac{8+2}{25} = \frac{10}{25}$
∴ B

Q3
Answer : (C)
Category : Graphs and Data Analysis
Explanation

그래프를 보면 3년이 지날 때까지는 전체적으로 sales가 increase하다가 4년차부터 decrease하기 시작한다. 따라서 3년차인 2000년도까지는 increase하고 그 다음부터 decrease하는 내용을 보기에서 찾으면 된다.
∴ C

Q4
Answer : (C)
Category : Graphs and Data Analysis, Functions
Explanation

Linear function이라고 했으므로
$f(n) = y = an + b$라고 하면,
$f(1) = a + b = -2$
$f(2) = 2a + b = 1$
$a = 3, \ b = -5 \ \rightarrow \ f(n) = 3n - 5$
∴ C

Q5
Answer : (B)
Category : Percentage
Explanation

562 juniors 중에 7%가 inducted되었으므로
$562 \times \frac{7}{100} = 39.34 \cong 39$
602 seniors 중에 5%가 inducted되었으므로
$602 \times \frac{5}{100} = 30.1 \cong 30$
$39 + 30 = 69$
∴ B

Q6
Answer : (A)
Category : Equations
Explanation

$(3x^2 - 5x + 2) + (5x^2 - 2x - 6)$
$= 8x^2 - 7x - 4$
∴ A

Q7
Answer : (D)
Category : Fractions
Explanation

$\frac{3}{5}w = \frac{4}{3} \rightarrow 9w = 20 \rightarrow w = \frac{20}{9}$

∴ D

Q8
Answer : (C)
Category : Equations, Functions
Explanation

$y = 0.56x + 27.2$가 linear function이고 x years 마다 0.56의 student가 increase하고 있는 것을 알 수 있다.

∴ C

Q9
Answer : (B)
Category : Rate
Explanation

4 minutes $= 4 \times 60 = 240$ seconds

25 m를 13.7 seconds에 walk한다고 했으므로

$25 : 13.7 = x : 240 \rightarrow x \cong 437.9 \cong 450$m

∴ B

Q10
Answer : (D)
Category : Graphs and Data Analysis, Equations
Explanation

$W = mg = 90 \times 3.6 = 324$

∴ D

Q11
Answer : (B)
Category : Ratio, Graphs and Data Analysis
Explanation

$W = mg = 9.8m = 150 \rightarrow m = \frac{150}{9.8}$kg

170 Newton이 되어야 하므로

$W = mg = \frac{150}{9.8} \times g = 170$

$\rightarrow g = 170 \times \frac{9.8}{150} = 11.1$m/s^2

∴ B

Q12
Answer : (D)
Category : Functions
Explanation

Five distinct zeros가 있으므로 그래프에서 distinct한 x-intercept가 5개 있어야 한다.

∴ D

Q13
Answer : (D)
Category : Equations
Explanation

$h = -16t^2 + vt + k \rightarrow vt = h - k + 16t^2$

$\rightarrow v = \frac{h-k}{t} + 16t$

∴ D

Q14
Answer : (A)
Category : Ratio, Equations
Explanation

$0.2 per MINUTE라고 했으므로 per HOUR로 바꾼다면 $c = ($0.2 \times 60) \times h$

∴ A

Q15

Answer : (A)

Category : Graphs and Data Analysis

Explanation

Experiment가 conclusive하기 위해서는 population이 well-defined되어야 하고, participant가 randomly selected되어야 한다. 이 experiment는 위의 조건을 만족시키므로 Treatment X는 효과가 있다고 할 수 있다.

∴ A

Q16

Answer : (B)

Category : Functions

Explanation

$f(-2) = -2$
$g(-2) = 2$
$f(-2) + g(-2) = 0$

∴ B

Q17

Answer : (B)

Category : Ratio, Functions

Explanation

$S(P) = \dfrac{1}{2}P + 40$

$D(P) = 220 - P$

P가 10 increase하면 $S(P)$는 $\dfrac{1}{2}P = 5$ increase 한다.

∴ B

Q18

Answer : (B)

Category : Equations, Functions

Explanation

$S(P) = D(P) = \dfrac{1}{2}P + 40 = 220 - P$

$P + 80 = 440 - 2P$

$3P = 360 \rightarrow P = 120$

∴ B

Q19

Answer : (C)

Category : Ratio

Explanation

1 ounce가 7 football field를 cover할 수 있고 1 football field는 $1\dfrac{1}{3} = \dfrac{4}{3}$ acre이므로 1 ounce 는 $7 \times \dfrac{4}{3}$ acre를 cover한다.

따라서 48 ounce는 $48 \times 7 \times \dfrac{4}{3} = 448$ acres를 cover할 수 있다.

∴ C

Q20

Answer : (B)

Category : Graphs and Data Analysis

Explanation

34 minutes coordinate을 보면 line of best fit에서의 heart rate는 150이고 실제 coordinate은 148이므로 그 차이는 2 beats per minute.

∴ B

Q21

Answer : (C)

Category : Functions

Explanation

Successive year마다 initial saving의 fixed percentage를 더하는 것은 전부 linear한 function 이다. "current value"의 percentage를 점차적으로 더하는 것이 exponential function이다.

∴ C

Q22

Answer : (B)

Category : Percentage, Equations

Explanation

세 number를 x, y, z라고 하면

$x+y+z=855$

$x=1.5(y+z) \rightarrow y+z=\dfrac{2}{3}x$

$x+\dfrac{2}{3}x=855 \rightarrow \dfrac{5}{3}x=855 \rightarrow x=513$

$\therefore$ B

Q23

Answer : (C)

Category : Trigonometry

Explanation

$\sin a = \cos(90-a)$이므로

$a+b=4k-22+6k-13=90 \rightarrow k=12.5$

$\therefore$ C

Q24

Answer : (D)

Category : Divisibility, Equations

Explanation

Number of students를 x라고 하면

$3x+5=n$

$4x-21=n$

$3x+5=4x-21 \rightarrow x=26$

$\therefore$ D

Q25

Answer : (D)

Category : Solids

Explanation

$V_{silo} = V_{cone} \times 2 + V_{cylinder}$

$= 2 \times \left(\dfrac{1}{3}\pi r^2 h_{cone}\right) + \pi r^2 h_{cylinder}$

$= 2 \times \left(\dfrac{1}{3}\pi \times 5^2 \times 5\right) + \pi \times 5^2 \times 10$

$= \dfrac{250\pi}{3} + 250\pi = \dfrac{1000\pi}{3} \cong 1047.2$

$\therefore$ D

Q26

Answer : (C)

Category : Functions

Explanation

Origin을 지나므로 $y=ax$라고 할 수 있다.

$k=2a$

$32=ak$

$\rightarrow 32=a(2a)=2a^2 \rightarrow a=\pm 4, k=\pm 8$

$\therefore$ C

Q27

Answer : (C)

Category : Perimeter and Area

Explanation

원래의 length를 l, width를 w라고 하면

원래의 area $= lw$

새로운 length $= 1.1l$

새로운 width $= \left(1-\dfrac{p}{100}\right)w$

새로운 area $= (1.1l)\left(1-\dfrac{p}{100}\right)w = 0.88lw$

$\rightarrow 1.1\left(1-\dfrac{p}{100}\right)lw = 0.88lw$

$\rightarrow 1.1\left(1-\dfrac{p}{100}\right) = 0.88$

$\rightarrow \dfrac{p}{100} = 1 - \dfrac{0.88}{1.1}$

$\rightarrow p = 20$

$\therefore$ C

Q28

Answer : (D)

Category : Functions

Explanation

20년마다 10% decrease이므로 t년 후를 계산하려면 $\dfrac{t}{20}$가 exponent가 되어야 한다.

또한 10% decrease이므로 남은 population은 0.9이므로 0.9가 base가 되어야 한다.

∴ D

Q29

Answer : (A)

Category : Probability, Graphs and Data Analysis, Equations

Explanation

	Handedness	
Gender	Left	Right
Female	x	$5x$
Male	y	$9y$
total	18	122

문제에서 주어진 조건을 table에 옮기면 위와 같다.

$x+y=18$

$5x+9y=122$

$\rightarrow x=10,\ y=8$

$\text{Probability}=\dfrac{\text{Right Handed Females}}{\text{Total Right Handed Students}}$

$=\dfrac{5x}{122}=\dfrac{50}{122}\cong 0.410$

∴ A

Q30

Answer : (A)

Category : Equations

Explanation

$3x+b=5x-7$

$3y+c=5y-7$

$b=2x-7$

$c=2y-7$

$b-c=2(x-y)=\dfrac{1}{2}\ \rightarrow\ x-y=\dfrac{1}{4}$

∴ A

Q31

Answer : 4 or 5

Category : Equations

Explanation

문제에서 주어진 조건들을 식으로 표현하면

$11\leq 2x+3\leq 14\ \rightarrow\ 4\leq x\leq 5.5$

x는 positive integer 이므로 $x=4,\ 5$

∴ 4 or 5

Q32

Answer : 58.6

Category : Statistics, Graphs and Data Analysis

Explanation

$\text{Mean}=\dfrac{\text{Sum of all ages of Presidents}}{\text{Number of Presidents}}$

$=\dfrac{57+62+58+58+59+58+62+55+68+51+50+65}{12}$

$\cong 58.6$

∴ 58.6

Q33

Answer : 9

Category : Equations

Explanation

$(-3x^2+5x-2)-2(x^2-2x-1)$

$=-3x^2+5x-2-2x^2+4x+2$

$=-5x^2+9x=ax^2+bx+c$

∴ $b=9$

Q34

Answer : $\dfrac{5}{8}$ or .625

Category : Circles

Explanation

Area of Sector는 central angle에 proportional 하다. 전체 circle의 angle=360°=2π rad이므로

$$\text{Area of Sector} = \text{Area of circle} \times \dfrac{\dfrac{5}{4}\pi}{2\pi}$$

$$= \text{Area of circle} \times \dfrac{5}{8}$$

∴ $\dfrac{5}{8}$ or .625

Q35

Answer : 50

Category : Statistics

Explanation

$$\text{Mean} = \dfrac{\text{Sum of data}}{\text{Number of Data}}$$

First 10 ratings의 average가 75라고 했으므로 Sum of the first 10 ratings=$75 \times 10 = 750$

20 ratings의 average가 85로 유지되려면 Total sum이 $85 \times 20 = 1700$이 되어야 한다.

따라서 $1700 - 750 = 950$

= total sum of ratings 11~20

11th rating의 least값이 되려면 남은 9 ratings가 전부 100을 줄 경우를 계산하여

$950 - 100 \times 9 = 50$

따라서 rating이 최소 50은 되어야 average of 85가 유지된다.

∴ 50

Q36

Answer : 750

Category : Equations, Functions

Explanation

$y \leq -15x + 3000$

$y \leq 5x$

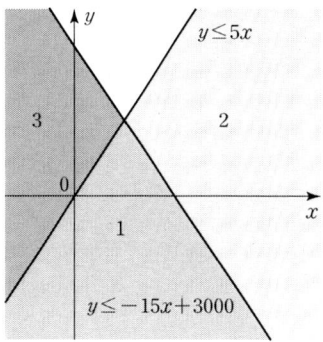

문제에서 주어진 조건을 그림으로 그리면 1번 영역에 해당되는 부분이 두 조건을 만족시키는 부분이다. 따라서 b의 maximum value를 구하면 $5x = -15x + 3000$

→ $x = 150$, $y = 750$ → $b = 750$

∴ 750

Q37

Answer : 7

Category : Rate, Equations

Explanation

$N = rT$

84 shoppers per hour이므로 per minute으로 convert하면 $\dfrac{84}{60}$ shoppers per minute이 된다.

따라서 $N = rT = \dfrac{84}{60} \times 5 = 7$ shoppers

∴ 7

Q38

Answer : 60

Category : Fractions, Rate, Equations

Explanation

90 shoppers per hour이므로 per minute으로 convert하면 $\dfrac{90}{60}$ shoppers per minute이 된다.

따라서 $N = rT = \dfrac{90}{60} \times 12 = 18$ shoppers

Original Store에서는 45 shoppers이므로 percentage를 구하면

$$\dfrac{45 - 18}{45} \times 100 = 60\%$$

∴ 60

Part 4

Practice Test #4

Practice Test #4

Section 1. Reading Test

Passage I. "The Balloonist"

Passage Summary

Lines

1-10: I am not sure how to explain the reasons for my passion.
10-19: My whole life has driven me to this goal of exploration, and I am helpless against it.
20-27: I am freely choosing to go wherever this adventure takes me.
28-41: I don't know why I'm choosing to go to the North Pole, since it is not useful. Perhaps only because it is difficult, and humans want to do impossible things and learn about the unknown.
42-49: And on top of that, it isn't even as if the Pole is interesting. It isn't. It is just an arbitrary place.
49-end: But here I am anyway, heading toward the North Pole, leaving civilization behind. I am not going in order to find knowledge or adventure. I am going to find myself, whether I like myself or not.

Main Idea

I am going on an adventure to the North Pole, because I must find myself.

Tone

Impassioned, first-person, contemplative

Vocabulary

| Line 2 | readily | a. 손쉽게, 순조롭게 |
| Line 2 | verifiable | a. 증명할 수 있는, 입증할 수 있는 |

Line 2	yearning	n. 갈망, 동경
Line 4	consummation	n. 완성
Line 7	is borne in upon	~에게 자각되다[분명해지다]
Line 9	undertaking	n. (중요한, 힘든) 일, 프로젝트
Line 12	clockwork	n. (시계의) 태엽장치
Line 14	sustenance	n. (음식, 물 등) 생명을 건강하게 유지시켜 주는 것, 자양분
Line 15	uninhabited	a. 사람이 살지 않는, 무인의
Line 18	cache	n. 은닉처
Line 19	cairn	n. (돌을 쌓아 만든) 이정표, 돌무덤
Line 21	will	v. 결정하다(determine)
Line 24	knot	n. 노트 (선박, 항공기의 속도를 재는 단위)
Line 28	intent	a. 강한 관심[흥미]를 보이는, 열중하는
Line 32	pulpit	n. 설교단, 단상
Line 32	expedition	n. 탐험, 원정(대)
Line 38	condemned to	~해야만 하도록 운명 지어진
Line 40	unthinking	a. 생각이 없는, 경솔한
Line 40	lust	n. (특히 애정이 동반되지 않은 강한) 성욕[욕정]
Line 46	featureless	a. 특색 없는
Line 46	wasteland	n. 황무지, 불모지
Line 47	abstraction	n. 관념, 추상적 개념
Line 51	trotting	a. 빨리 걷는
Line 53	bedstead	n. 침대틀 (침대의 프레임)
Line 54	volition	n. 자유의지
Line 56	on the brink of	~의 직전에 (있는)
Line 57	ephemeral	a. 수명이 짧은, 단명하는; 덧없는
Line 60	egotism	n. 자기중심적인 습관
Line 61	surrender	n. 굴복, 양도

Questions

Q1 THING: Main Idea, Tone

Answer Key : (C)

Lines 9–10에서 "my motives in this undertaking are not entirely clear"이라고 하면서 자기가 왜 North Pole로 가고 싶은지 uncertain하다. 하지만 lines 56–57에 가서는 자기 journey 때문에 North Pole에 대하여가 아니라, 자기 자신에 대하여 더 잘 알게 된다고 한다. 즉 uncertainty에서 recognition으로 shift하고 있다.

Eliminate

(A), (B), (D) fears going on the expedition, 자기 ability에 대한 doubt, 또는 North Pole에 대한 disdain은 not mentioned

Q2 THING: Line Evidence

Answer Key : (D)

1번 문제에 대한 답의 keywords인 "uncertainty of motives", "recognition of [motives]"가 subject로 나오는 lines를 찾아보자. Lines 56-57에서 "What I am on the brink of knowing, I now see, is not an ephemeral mathematical spot but myself"라고 말하면서 자기가 왜 North Pole로 가는지 recognize한다.

Eliminate

(A), (B), (C) 모두 North Pole에 가는 이유보다 준비하는 과정과 expectations를 설명

Q3 THING: Vocabulary

Answer Key : (D)

Lines 1-6에서 narrator가 "vast yearning"을 가지고 있지만, 자기도 "not understand ... what it is that the yearning desires"라고 한다. Narrator도 자기 감정을 완전히 이해하기 어려움 → 자기 감정이 "not readily verifiable"이라는 것은 not understood라는 의미이다.

Eliminate

(A), (B), (C) incorrect in context

Q4 THING: Main Idea

Answer Key : (C)

Lines 10-13에서 narrator는 destiny가 자기를 North Pole로 이끌고 있다고 말한다. 즉 자기가 control할 수 없는 강한 force가 자기를 influence하고 있다고 말한다.

Second best answer: (D)

Lines 10-13에서 그런 forces들이 "years, for a lifetime" 동안 자기를 influence하고 있었다고 말하지만, 그것이 main focus는 아님

Eliminate

(A) destiny가 "in secret"으로 work했다고 하지만, narrator가 hide한 것은 아님

(B) destiny가 clockwork같다고 하지만, narrator가 methodical하다는 내용 not mentioned

(D) main focus가 아님

Q5 THING: Problem

Answer Key : (A)

Lines 20–21에서 "Nobody has succeeded in this thing, and many have died"라고 하는 것을 볼 때 North Pole로 가다가 많은 사람들이 죽었다는 것을 알 수 있다.

Eliminate

(B), (C), (D) previous explorer들이 만든 surprising discovery, North Pole의 location을 찾지 못하는 것, different motivations는 not mentioned

Q6 THING: Line Evidence

Answer Key : (A)

5번 문제에 대한 답의 keywords인 "previous explorers", "perished"가 나오는 lines를 찾아보자. Lines 20–21에서 "many have died"라고 하면서 explorer들의 죽음을 mention하고 있다.

Eliminate

(B), (C), (D) keywords가 나오지 않음

Q7 THING: Tone, Contrasting Pairs

Answer Key : (B)

Narrator는 자기 journey에 "intent"하면서도, lines 27–39에서 그런 journey가 absurd하다는 것을 인정한다. "Who wants the North Pole! What good is it! Can you eat it?" 이런 질문들을 통해서 North Pole은 practical value가 없다는 것을 보여준다. 하지만 결국에는 "must nevertheless be sought for"이라고 말하면서 꼭 가야겠다고 한다.

Eliminate:

(A), (D) absurd하게 생각하기는 하지만, immoral하다는 내용, scientifically important하다는 내용 not mentioned

(C) passage는 오히려 socially beneficial하지 않다는 것을 강조

Q8 THING: Question

Answer Key : (D)

Lines 27–39에서 "Who wants the North Pole! What good is it! Can you eat it?" 이런 질문들을 통해서 North Pole은 사람들에게 구체적인 benefit을 주지 않는다는 것을 보여준다.

Eliminate

(A), (B), (C) North Pole을 간다고 railway처럼 이동할 수 있는 practical benefit이 있지 않다는 얘기는 했지만, 그렇다고 trains나 travel이 main focus는 아님

Q9 THING: Main Idea, Point of View

Answer Key : (D)

Lines 48–49에서 North Pole에 "no one but a Swedish madman could take the slightest interest in it"이라고 함 → "take the slightest interest in"은 curious해 하고 관심 가지는 것을 말한다.

Eliminate

(A), (B), (C) incorrect meaning in context

Q10 THING: Vocabulary

Answer Key : (A)

Lines 49–51에서 narrator는 자기가 North Pole로 가는 것을 describe하고 있다: "The wind is still from the south, bearing us steadily northward at the speed of a trotting dog." 여기서 "bearing"은 바람이 narrator를 carry한다는 의미로 쓰이고 있다.

Eliminate

(B), (C) incorrect in meaning

(D) incorrect meaning in context

Passage II. "The Great Inversion and the Future of the American City"

Passage Summary

Lines

1-11: People aren't actually moving back to the cities like some say. Trends are mixed. Only the population of cities in the South and Southwest increased.

12-19: The biggest trends were that African Americans moved out of city centers and immigrants moved to the suburbs.

20-28: Wealthy professionals moved to the cities. The wealthy populations stayed the same in these places during financial crisis years, though unemployment increased in the suburbs. Not many moved because a few new apartment buildings were being built.

28-35: However, the switching of populations will probably start again, because these population switches are happening in every kind of city.

36-47: Cities are having difficulty meeting their financial responsibilities, but data shows that it doesn't seem to be making rich professionals move away.

48-53: The flight of wealthy professionals away from cities seems to be ending, and we need to adjust policy to fit those circumstances.

54-63: Our modern conception of city zones come from a paper written in 1925.

64-71: That paper was right in 1925 and in 1974: most cities looked the same, with a busy downtown, industrial areas, worker residences near them, and wealthy homes outside the city.

72-79: During that time, as people became wealthier, they moved further and further out of the city.

80-92: However, that isn't true anymore. Since there are no factories anymore to make living in the city uncomfortable, now the wealthy live in the city and the poor live outside.

Main Idea

Rich and poor populations in cities are being inverted due to the changes in the way our industrial system works. The poor are moving out, and the rich are moving in, which is the opposite of how it was.

Tone

Informative, neutral

Vocabulary

Line 1	abandonment	n. 버림, 포기
Line 3	census	n. 인구조사
Line 4	turn up	v. 가리키다, 나타내다
Line 4	stampede	n. (사람, 동물들이 한쪽으로) 우르르 몰림, 쇄도
Line 7	albeit	conj. 비록 ~일지라도
Line 7	increment	n. (수, 양의) 증가
Line 12	demographic	a. 인구(통계)학의
Line 12	inversion	n. (위치, 순서 등의) 도치[전도], 뒤바뀜
Line 12	raw	a. (통계자료로 쓰기 위해 세밀하게) 가공을 하지 않은
Line 13	blunt	a. 무딘, 둔한
Line 20	affluent	a. 부유한
Line 22	recession	n. 불경기, 불황
Line 27	condo	n. (미국의) 아파트
Line 29	prevailing	a. 우세한, 지배적인
Line 30	bust	n. 실패, 쇠락 (여기서는 건설경기가 추락한 것을 말함)
Line 30	once that	(일단) ~하기만 하면
Line 32	proxy	n. (측정, 계산하려는 다른 것을 대표하도록 이용하는) 대용물
Line 35	undergoing	a. 겪다
Line 35	modest	a. (아주 대단하지는 않은) 보통의
Line 36	fiscal	a. 재정적인
Line 37	public pension	n. 공적 연금
Line 38	incur	v. (어떤 좋지 못한 상황을) 초래하다
Line 43	entitled	a. 자격이 있는
Line 53	mobility	n. (사회적) 유동성
Line 63	enclave	n. (한 국가나 도시 내의) 소수의 거주지
Line 71	continuum	n. 연속체 (여기서는 그 앞에서 언급한 연속된 거주영역을 뜻함)
Line 74	spacious	a. (방, 건물이) 널찍한
Line 76	bore resemblance to	~을 닮았다
Line 84	close–in	a. 가까운 거리의, 인접한
Line 86	submerged	a. 수몰[침수]된; 최저 생활을 하는, 극빈층의
Line 87	degradation	n. 비하, 수모; 악화
Line 90	accumulate	v. (서서히) 모으다, 축적하다

Questions

Q11 THING: Main Idea

Answer Key : (C)

Lines 32–33에서 "demographic inversion is not a proxy for population growth"라고 말하면서 둘을 따로 분리시킨다. 또한 lines 33–35에서 demographic inversion이 "can occur in cities that are growing, those whose numbers are flat, and even in those undergoing a modest decline in size"라고 말하는 것으로 보아 demographic inversion이 많은 곳에서 일어난다고 볼 수 있다.

Eliminate

(A), (B), (D) 첫 문단을 summarize하지 않음

Q12 THING: Main Idea

Answer Key : (D)

Lines 14–17에서 "The most powerful demographic events"가 "movement of African Americans out of central cities"라고 말한다.

Eliminate

(A), (B), (C) unemployed, immigrants, 또는 young professionals가 central-city area에서 move away한다는 것은 not mentioned

Q13 THING: Vocabulary

Answer Key : (A)

Lines 33–35에서 democratic inversion은 "in cities that are growing"과 "those whose numbers are flat"에 둘 다 일어날 수 있다고 한다. 즉 여기서 "flat"은 숫자가 변하지 않는 것이다.

Eliminate

(B), (C), (D) incorrect meaning in context

Q14 THING: Problem

Answer Key : (B)

Lines 36–39에서 city들이 "past two decades"에 만든 "public pension obligations"를 더 이상 pay하지 못해서 economic hardship을 겪고 있다고 한다. Lines 41–43에서도 Chicago를 예로 들어 사람들이 당연히 생각하는 "public services"를 afford하지 못한다고 한다.

Eliminate

(A), (C), (D) tax increases, inner-city tax base, manufacturing production과 경제적 status의 관계에 대한 내용 not mentioned

Q15 THING: Line Evidence

Answer Key : (A)

Lines 36–39에서 keyword "fiscal problems"가 "public pension obligations"의 result라는 것을 볼 수 있다. 즉 옛날에 했던 약속들과 "public pension obligations" 때문에 지금 economic hardship을 겪고 있다고 말해 준다.

Eliminate

(B), (C), (D) keywords가 subject로 나오지 않음

Q16 THING: List

Answer Key : (C)

Lines 54–63에서 Ernest W. Burgess가 도시들을 4개의 zones로 나누는 것에 대해서 얘기한다. 또한, lines 66–71에서 그 zones에 대해서 더 자세히 설명한다: "every city ... had a downtown ... it had a factory district just beyond: it had districts of working class residences just beyond that: and it had residential suburbs for the wealthy." 또한, line 65에서 그런 four-zone structure는 "urban America of 1974"에도 있었다고 얘기한다

Eliminate

(A), (B), (D) flight of minority populations to the suburbs, lose manufacturing sectors, experiencing demographic inversions에 대한 내용 not mentioned

Q17 THING: Line Evidence

Answer Key : (C)

Lines 66–71에서 1974년에 미국은 four-zone structure라는 것을 자세히 설명한다.

Eliminate

(A) American cities의 layout을 설명하는 seminal paper에 대한 내용

(B) Burgess가 만든 이론을 설명하고 있지만, 그것이 1974년에 어떻게 support되었는지 설명하지 않음

(D) suburb로 옮기는 것에 focus

Q18 THING: Vocabulary

Answer Key : (A)

Lines 66–68에서 1974년에 American cities들은 다 downtown이 있어서, 여기서 "commercial life of the metropolis was conducted"라고 함 → context 상 "conducted"는 business를 carry out하는 것이다.

Eliminate

(B) incorrect meaning in context

(C), (D) incorrect meaning

Q19 THING: Graph

Answer Key : (B)

Chart 1은 2010년에 non-metro, small metro, 그리고 large metro areas에서 살았던 미국 사람들의 %를 보여준다. 즉 census number들을 나타내고 있다. Author는 lines 11-13에서 "raw census numbers"가 "ineffective blunt instrument"라고 말한다. 즉 author는 Chart 1에 나오는 data가 "ineffective blunt instrument"라고 생각할 것이다.

Eliminate

(A), (C) author는 census data를 크게 신뢰하지 않을 것임
(D) census data가 완벽하지 못하다고 주장하지만, chart에 나오는 정보와 disagree하지는 않음

Q20 THING: Graph

Answer Key : (A)

Chart 2에서 1990s에 large, small, non-metro areas 모두 2000s보다 훨씬 많이 성장했다는 것을 보여준다. Large metro는 1990s에 14%, 2000s에 10.9% 성장했고, small metro는 1990s에 13.1%, 2000s에 10.3% 성장했다. Non-metro areas는 1990s에 9.0%, 2000s에 4.5% 성장했다. 즉 2000s에는 모든 metropolitan areas들이 1990s에 비해서 덜 성장했다.

Eliminate

(B), (C), (D) not supported by chart

Q21 THING: Graph

Answer Key : (D)

Chart 2에서 1990s에 large, small, non-metro areas 모두 1980s 보다 성장했다는 것을 보여준다. Large metro는 1980s에 12.5%, 1990s에 14% 성장했고, small metro는 1980s에 8.8%, 1990s에 13.1% 성장했다. Non-metro areas는 1980s에 1.8%, 1990s에 9.0% 성장했다. 즉 1980s metropolitan areas는 모두 1990s에 비해 덜 성장했다.

Eliminate

(A), (B), (C) not supported by chart

Passage III. "Frankenstein's Cat"

Passage Summary

Lines

1-11: When the genome was first mapped, scientists wanted to use it to manipulate animal DNA to help humans, which was called 'pharming'.

12-19: Using proteins created by our own body to make medicine seems like a good idea, but it is difficult to mass produce such proteins.

20-30: Dairy animals can make proteins very well, so scientists researched how to manipulate the animals' cells to produce those chemicals in the animal's milk.

31-53: At first the idea was only fantasy, but when GTC Biotherapeutics created ATryn, it became a reality after they used genetically modified goats to make protein. The protein helps prevent deadly blood clots in people who can't make it on their own.

54-end: In order to do it, they injected the gene into goat eggs, and injected the eggs into mother goats. When the goats were born, some of them carried the gene and a strand of DNA called a 'promoter', the promoter caused the gene to activate when they produced milk, which produced the protein. The farm is very effective at mass–producing the protein.

Main Idea

It used to be a dream to modify animals to produce helpful substances for humans, but now it is a reality after a company used goats to produce helpful protein.

Tone

Informative, Neutral

Vocabulary

Line 2	genome	n.	게놈 (세포나 생명체의 유전자를 통틀어 부르는 말)
Line 5	envision	v.	(특히 앞으로 바라는 일을) 마음 속에 그리다
Line 6	consequential	a.	중대한
Line 9	pharming	n.	여기서는 '유전공학으로 가공된 동물들을 사육'하는 것을 뜻함
Line 10	tweak	n.	약간의 수정, 변경
Line 11	pharmaceutical	a.	약학의, 제약의
Line 12	crank out		(빠르게) 만들어 내다, 양산하다

Line 14	enzyme	n. 효소
Line 14	hormone	n. 호르몬
Line 14	clot	v. (혈액을) 엉기게 하다, 응고시키다
Line 14	antibody	n. 항체
Line 16	autoimmune	a. 자가면역(의)
Line 21	udder	n. (암소, 염소 등의) 젖통
Line 21	swollen	a. 부어 오른, 부풀어오른
Line 22	*transgenic*	a. 이식 유전자를 가진
Line 34	therapeutic	a. 치료의, 치료법의
Line 35	gee–whiz	a. 깜짝 놀랄만한
Line 36	geekery	n. 괴짜
Line 39	antithrombin	n. 안티트롬빈, 항트롬빈
Line 39	anticoagulant	n. 혈액응고방지제, 항응혈제
Line 42	bouncer	n. 원래 클럽 앞에서 기준에 맞지 않는 사람이 들어오지 못하게 통제하는 사람을 뜻하며, 여기서는 혈액 속에서 그런 역할을 하는 요소를 말함
Line 43	sidling up to	~에 쭈뼛쭈뼛/슬금슬금 다가가서
Line 45	mutation	n. 돌연변이
Line 47	prone	a. (좋지 않은 일을) 당하기 쉬운
Line 50	supplemental	a. 추가의, 보충의 (supplementary)
Line 55	microinjection	n. 현미경 수준에서 아주 극소량의 주사
Line 56	GloFish	관상용 열대어 제브라피시의 유전자조작으로 만든 인공 관상어. 빛의 종류에 따라 다른 색을 띤다.
Line 56	AquAdvantage salmon	Atlantic salmon의 유전자변형 연어. 1년 반 만에 성체가 되어 자연산 연어 수량증대에 도움이 된다.
Line 58	fertilized	a. 수태한
Line 59	womb	n. 자궁
Line 61	nestle	v. (아늑한 곳에) 자리잡다
Line 63	promoter	n. 촉진제
Line 65	mammary gland	a. 젖샘, 유선
Line 66	*lactate*	v. 젖을 내다[분비하다]
Line 70	Et voilà	(프랑스어) '짜잔! 이제 됐어! / 완성이야!'라는 뜻
Line 73	parlor	n. ~하는 방, 장소. Miling parlor는 '착유실' 정도로 생각하면 되겠다.

Questions

Q22 THING: Main Idea

Answer Key : (A)

Lines 9–11에서 "Welcome to the world of 'pharming,' in which simple genetic tweaks turn animals into living pharmaceutical factories"라고 main point를 보여준다. 그 후에 pharming의 발달 과정과 ATryn이라는 약을 설명한다.

Eliminate

(B) research한다는 것은 나오지만 그것을 자세히 설명하거나 main focus로 두지 않음

(C) results만 summarize하는 것이 아니라 그런 발견을 하기까지의 과정도 나옴

(D) development는 맞지만 branch of scientific study는 아님

Q23 THING: Tone

Answer Key : (C)

Passage에서 pharming에 대한 비판적인 내용이 없으며, author는 전체적으로 긍정적이다. Line 70에서 pharming의 결과에 대해 "Voila – human medicine!"이라고 즐겁게 외친다. 즉 author는 appreciative하다.

Eliminate

(A), (B), (D) fear, discontent, surprise는 not mentioned

Q24 THING: Vocabulary

Answer Key : (C)

Lines 19–21에서 dairy animals는 "expert protein producers"라고 한다. 즉 여기서 expert는 capable하다는 것이다.

Eliminate

(A), (B) 소 같은 dairy animals들이 protein을 만들지만 그것에 대해서 knowledgeable하거나 professional하지 않음

(D) dairy animal들이 우유를 만드는 것은 trained된 것이 아니라 원래 할 수 있는 것임

Q25 THING: Transition word, List

Answer Key : (B)

Line 36에서 처음 pharming 실험들은 "lab–bound thought experiments come true"라고 하면서, 사실 큰 benefit을 주기보다는 그냥 theoretical value만 있었다고 말한다. 그러므로 바로 사용할 수 있는 products를 만들 expectation은 없었다.

Eliminate

(A), (D) cost of animal research, molecular properties of certain animals는 not mentioned

(C) 모든 transgenic studies가 anticoagulants에만 집중되었다고 말하진 않음

Q26 THING: Line Evidence

Answer Key : (C)

Lines 35–36에서 첫 transgenic studies들을 productive하지 않다는 것을 보여주는 keywords를 찾아보자. "merely gee–whiz," "scientific geekery," 그리고 "lab–bound thought experiments come true" 모두 practical value가 없다는 것을 보여준다.

Eliminate

(A), (B) transgenic studies에 대한 내용 not mentioned

(D) ATryn에 focus

Q27 THING: Main Idea, Transition Word

Answer Key : (A)

Lines 42–44에서 ATryn을 "molecular bouncer, sidling up to clot–forming compounds and escorting them out of the bloodstream"로 describe한 것을 볼 때, 너무 많이 clot하지 않도록 막아준다는 것을 알 수 있다.

Eliminate

(B), (C), (D) rare genetic mutation, DNA sequence, 또는 염소 gland 안에 naturally 생긴다는 것은 not mentioned

Q28 THING: Line Evidence

Answer Key : (B)

Blood clot이 줄어드는 것을 보여주는 keywords를 찾자. Lines 44–46에서 "escorting them [clot–forming compounds] out"라고 하는 key phrase가 mention되었다.

Eliminate

(A), (C), (D) keywords가 not mentioned

Q29 THING: Main Idea, Contrasting Pair

Answer Key : (B)

Lines 60–62에서 염소들 중에 "some of them proved to be transgenic"이라고 했다. "some of them"이라는 말은 모두가 transgenic하지는 않다는 얘기다.

Eliminate

(A), (C), (D) female goat들이 antithrombin을 만드는 내용, 처음으로 microinjection 받았다는 내용, humans 안에 주로 genes가 있다는 내용 not mentioned

Q30 THING: Quotes

Answer Key : (D)

Lines 63–64에서 parentheses를 "promoter"라는 단어 바로 뒤에 넣었다. 즉 promoter가 무엇인지 define을 해 준다.

Eliminate

(A), (B), (C) parenthetical information의 의도와 관련 없음

Q31 THING: Quotes, Tone

Answer Key : (D)

"Gold"는 주로 economically 좋은 것을 describe할 때 쓰인다. 여기서도 ATryn을 "liquid gold"로 비유한 것은 그만큼 economically valuable하다고 설명하려고 한 것이다.

Eliminate

(A), (B), (C)에 나오는 microinjection, dairy production에서 efficiency, 그리고 dairy farmers한테 economically 좋은 것에 대한 내용 not mentioned

Passage IV. "Reflections on the Revolution in France" / "Rights of Man"

Passage 1

Passage Summary

Lines

1-16: Because weakness and uncertainty in our government is so bad, we should be afraid to question that government. We should be afraid of doing this even if we are trying to help.

17-24: A government is a contract between state and people, but it isn't a business contract to be cancelled or ignored whenever we want.

24-40: It is a deep and lasting partnership with considerations that go beyond ourselves, and extends to all our descendents and every consideration of humankind. Without it, we would have brutal chaos.

Main Idea

It is dangerous to challenge the established social order, because chaos and uncertainty are dangerous.

Tone

Persuasive, emphatic, passionate

Passage 2

Passage Summary

Lines

41-45: All people should be free to act as they see necessary for their time, and being forced to listen to past rules is tyrannical.

46-54: Just as one man cannot own another, so too can no past time control a different time.

55-63: Every time and generation needs to decide for itself what the best ways of living are, and the past has to be the past.

64-72: The past is dead, and the future not yet here. How can two non–existent things have a responsibility to each other?

73-80: Everything changes, and since government is only for the living, the living should be in charge and not the dead.

Main Idea

The present people must decide for itself the best way to govern, instead of relying on the rules of the past.

Tone

Persuasive, emphatic, passionate

Vocabulary

Line 1	inconstancy		n. 변하기 쉬움, 변덕스러움
Line 2	versatility		n. 융통성
Line 3	obstinacy		n. 완고함, 고집
Line 4	consecrate		v. (종교 의식을 통해) 축성하다, 짓다
Line 5	corruption		n. (특히 권위 있는 위치에 있는 사람들의) 부패, 타락
Line 5	due caution		적절한 주의(를 기울임)
Line 7	subversion		n. 전복, 파괴, 멸망
Line 9	pious		a. 경건한, 독실한
Line 9	trembling		a. 떨리는, 전율하는
Line 9	solicitude		n. 고독
Line 12	rashly		ad. 성급하게, 경솔히
Line 12	hack		v. (마구, 거칠게) 자르다, 베다
Line 14	incantation		n. (마술을 걸기 위한) 주문
Line 19	dissolve		v. 용해시키다; 끝내다, 없애다
Line 19	at pleasure		임의로
Line 21	calico		n. 캘리코 (날염을 한 거친 면직물)
Line 24	be looked on		관망된다, 여겨진다
Line 25	reverence		n. 숭배
Line 26	subservient		a. ~에 굴종하는; (~보다) 부차적인, 덜 중요한
Line 27	perishable		a. 잘 상하는, 썩는
Line 34	municipal		a. 지방 자치제의, 시[읍/군]의
Line 36	speculation		n. 추측, (어림)짐작
Line 37	contingent		a. (~의) 여부에 따른
Line 38	asunder		ad. 산산이, 뿔뿔이

Line 43	vanity	n. 자만심, 허영심
Line 43	presumption	n. 추정; 주제넘음, 건방짐
Line 45	insolent	a. 버릇없는, 무례한
Line 49	dispose of	~을 없애다, 처리하다
Line 58	accommodate	v. 수용하다
Line 59	cease	v. 중단되다, 그치다
Line 63	how administered	어떻게 관리되는지
Line 67	conceive	v. 상상하다, 품다; 임신하다
Line 69	nonentity	n. 별 볼 일 없는 사람, 보잘것없는 사람

Questions

Q32 THING: Contrasting Pair

Answer Key : (D)

Lines 25–29에 Burke는 사람과 society 사이의 contract가 "temporary and perishable" 한 것과의 partnership이 아니라고 묘사한다. 즉 permanence를 강조하고 있다. 또 "all science", "all art", "every virtue and in all perfection"의 partnership이라고 찬양하면서 그 seriousness를 강조하고 있다.

Eliminate

(A) line 27에서 "temporary"하지 않다고 함 → brief하지 않음

(B), (C) complexity나 precision을 비교하지 않음

Q33 THING: Vocabulary

Answer Key : (D)

Lines 1–9에서 Burke는 사람들이 state의 "defects or corruption"을 바로잡으려 하지 말아야 하고, "subversion"을 통해 reform하려하지 말아야 한다고 주장 → context 상 state는 political entity나 government를 의미한다.

Eliminate

(A), (B), (C) incorrect in context

Q34 THING: Vocabulary

Answer Key : (A)

Lines 17–29에서 Burke가 state는 "a partnership agreement in a trade … or some other such low concern"이 아니라고 함 → context 상 "low"는 크게 중요하지 않은 petty concerns를 말한다.

Eliminate

(B), (C), (D) incorrect in context

Q35 THING: Point of View, Quotes

Answer Key : (D)

Lines 41–43에서 Paine은 "Every age and generation must be free to act for itself, in all cases,"라고 말하고, lines 61–63에서 죽은 사람들은 authority가 있으면 안 된다고 함 → context 상 past generation이 modern life의 결정에 영향을 미치면 안 된다고 주장한다.

Eliminate

(A) Paine은 past generations에 대해 긍정적인 말을 하지 않음

(B) difficulty not mentioned

(C) not the main focus

Q36 THING: Point of View, Contrasting Pairs

Answer Key : (B)

Lines 30–34에서 Burke는 옛 세대와 지금 세대의 partnership을 강조하지만, Paine은 옛 세대는 지금 세대를 control하면 안 된다고 주장한다.

Eliminate

(A), (C), (D) lines 30–34의 main idea인 옛 세대와 지금 세대의 partnership과 관련 없음

Q37 THING: Line Evidence

Answer Key : (D)

36번 문제에 대한 정답의 key phrases인 "politically meaningful links"와 "the dead, the living, and the unborn"가 등장하는 lines를 찾아보자. Lines 67–72에서 key phrases와 비슷한 뜻인 "possible obligation", "two nonentities, the one out of existence and the other not in"이 등장한다.

Eliminate

(A), (B), (C) key phrases가 등장하지 않음

Q38 THING: Point of View, Contrasting Pair

Answer Key : (D)

Lines 73–80에서 Paine은 social issues는 시간에 따라 변하므로, current generation은 past generation의 choices를 항상 따르려고 하면 안 된다고 한다. 하지만 lines 30–34를 보면 Burke는 dead와 yet to be born한 사람들과의 partnership인 government를 current generation이 마음대로 지금 바꾸면 안 된다고 생각한다는 것을 알 수 있다. 그러므로 Burke는 Paine의 마지막 argument를 disapprove했을 것이다.

Eliminate

(A) Burke와 Paine은 정반대의 의견을 가지고 있으므로, approve했을 가능성은 없음

(B), (C) resignation, skepticism은 Burke의 반응을 정확히 describe하지 못함

Q39 THING: Line Evidence

Answer Key : (D)

38번 문제의 key phrases인 "changing conditions"와 "changing the form of government"가 등장하는 lines를 찾아보자. Lines 34–38에서 key phrases와 비슷한 뜻인 "speculations of a contingent improvement", "separate and tear asunder the bands"가 등장한다. 즉 고작 "speculations"를 이유로 government를 마음대로 바꾸는 것을 반대하는 내용은 lines 34–38에 나온다.

Eliminate

(A), (B), (C) key phrases가 subject로 쓰이지 않았음

Q40 THING: Point of View, Contrasting Pairs

Answer Key : (A)

Passage 1: 사람들과 government 사이에는 reverent하게 여길 contract가 있고, past, current, 그리고 future generation 모두 이 contract에 포함된다고 주장한다. 즉 current와 future generation들 모두 past generation의 결정들을 따라야 한다.

Passage 2: current 및 future generation들은 past generation을 따를 의무가 없다고 주장한다. 그러므로, passage 2는 passage 1에서 말한 것을 challenge하고 있다.

Eliminate

(B), (C), (D) alternative approach, further evidence, attitude exemplifying은 not mentioned

Q41 THING: Main Idea

Answer Key : (B)

Passage 1에서는 government는 sacred하고, 사람들은 interfere하면 안 된다고 한다. 반면에 passage 2는 사람들은 자기 government를 바꿀 수 있다고 한다. 그러므로 두 passage 모두 government와 사람들의 relationship을 살피고 있다.

Eliminate

(A) resolve a particular struggle 에 대한 내용 not mentioned

(C) passage 1에서 political change를 빠르게 마음대로 하는 것을 반대하지만, main focus는 아님

(D) government의 duty보다는 사람들이 government와 관계가 어떻게 되어야 하는지 다루고 있음

Passage V. "Source of Medieval Eruption Identified"

Passage Summary

Lines
- **1-4:** Finding where the volcano which started the little Ice Age 750 years ago has been tricky.
- **5-16:** We know it happened, when it happened, and how strong it is. It sent a lot of sulfur into the air and blocked out the sun, causing the ice age.
- **17-32:** Scientists discovered geological evidence that a massive volcanic eruption triggered the ice age and then smaller ones afterward kept the cooling going.
- **33-42:** Some scientists think the big eruption happened in Indonesia, based on old documents found there.
- **43-54:** Based on this, they attempted to find the volcanic crater by surveying the rocks in the area. They found evidence that one of the largest volcanoes in our geological era erupted there.
- **55-60:** Evidence found in the geological layers also prove that the eruption must have happened in the 13th century, which is when the Little Ice Age happened.
- **61-67:** It makes sense that Indonesia was the site of the volcano because it is on the equator, which explains how sulfur from it could reach both poles.
- **68-end:** Another volcano in Ecuador is a possible candidate, but the Indonesian volcano has a closer match for the chemical composition of the ash layer, so scientists are convinced that it is responsible for the Little Ice Age.

Main Idea

Scientists found and compared a variety of geological data to confirm that an Indonesian volcano is the likely cause of the Little Ice Age in the 13th century.

Tone

Informative, neutral, scientific

Vocabulary

Line 3	cold snap	일시적 한파
Line 4	tricky	a. 다루기 힘든, 까다로운
Line 7	sulfate deposit	황산염 광상

Line 8	shard	n. (유리, 금속 등의) 조각, 파편
Line 10	stratosphere	n. 성층권
Line 11	climate-perturbing	a. 기후를 요동시키는
Line 13	Holocene	n. 홀로세[충적세] (약 1만 300년 전의 시대로, 지질시대의 최후 시대)
Line 14	haze	n. 연무, 실안개; 희뿌연 것
Line 17	geochemist	n. 지구화학자
Line 19	onset	n. (특히 불쾌한 일의) 시작
Line 20	radiocarbon	n. 방사성탄소
Line 22	sediment	n. 퇴적물
Line 24	abruptly	ad. 돌연히, 갑작스럽게
Line 25	intensified	a. (정도, 강도가) 심해진, 격렬해진
Line 28	subsequent	a. 그 다음의, 차후의(next)
Line 31	aerosol	n. 미립자로 된 것
Line 32	prolong	v. 연장시키다
Line 33	volcanologist	n. 화산학자
Line 38	Javanese	a. 자바 섬의
Line 38	catastrophically	ad. 대이변으로, 비극적으로
Line 39	devastate	v. (한 장소나 지역을) 완전히 파괴하다
Line 41	sweep	n. (완만하게 곡선을 이루며) 길게 펼쳐진 길. 여기서는 용암이 구불구불하게 흘러내리는 것을 뜻함
Line 42	pyroclastic	a. 화쇄암의, 화산 쇄설암으로 된
Line 44	caldera	n. 칼데라 (화산 폭발로 인해 화산 꼭대기가 거대하게 패여 생긴 부분)
Line 45	basin	n. 양푼 같이 생긴 그릇, 대야; 분지
Line 45	crater	n. 분화구, 큰 구멍
Line 46	outcrop	n. 노두 (광맥, 암석 등의 노출 부위)
Line 46	flank	n. (건물, 산 등의) 측면
Line 47	pumice	n. 부석, 속돌 (화산이 분출하여 생성된 암석의 한 종류)
Line 49	deposit	v. (서서히) 침전되다
Line 50	plume	n. (연기, 수증기 등이 피어오르는) 기둥
Line 52	explosivity	n. 폭발(성). Volcanic explosivity index 화산폭발지수
Line 63	equatorial	a. 적도의
Line 65	ice cap	n. (특히 극지방의) 만년설
Line 66	consensus	n. 공통점
Line 77	medieval	a. 중세의

> **Questions**

Q42 THING: Main Idea

Answer Key : (C)

Lines 1-3에서 어떠한 "powerful volcano"가 750년 전에 erupt한 후 "Little Ice Age"가 시작되었다고 한다. Lines 17-78에서는 volcano Samalas가 이 volcano였을 것이라는 과학자들의 주장과 왜 그렇게 생각하는지 설명하고 있다.

Eliminate

(A), (B), (D) passage에 부분적으로 나오는 specific detail이지, main purpose는 아님

Q43 THING: Main Idea

Answer Key : (B)

처음에는 Little Ice Age가 무엇인지 설명하고 나서, radiocarbon analysis로 어떻게 시작되었고 그런 eruption을 통해서 왜 추워졌는지 얘기하고 있다.

Eliminate

(A) scientific model을 비판하지 않음

(C) sulfate를 measure하는 새로운 방법을 제시하지 않음

(D) radiocarbon dating에서 volcanic glass로 가지 않음

Q44 THING: Line Evidence

Answer Key : (A)

43번 문제의 key phrases인 "a recorded event"와 "likely cause"가 등장하는 lines를 찾아보자. Lines 17-25에서 key phrases와 context상 같은 뜻인 "the cold summers... between 1275 and 1300 CE"와 "radiocarbon dating", "ice data", "sediment core data"가 등장한다.

Eliminate

(B), (C), (D) key phrases가 not mentioned

Q45 THING: Tone

Answer Key : (D)

Lines 5-8에서 volcano가 erupt했다는 evidence가 written in 되었다고 하면서 polar ice caps에서 evidence를 찾을 수 있다고 강조한다.

Eliminate

(A), (B), (C) hands-on nature of work, scientists write about discoveries, sense of importance about work에 대한 내용 not mentioned

Q46 THING: Main Idea

Answer Key : (A)

Lines 33–35에서 Indonesia에 있는 volcano Samalas가 erupt했다고 과학자들이 주장한다. 또한 lines 61–67에서 equator에 있으면 "consistent with the apparent climate impacts"할 수 있다고 주장한다.

Eliminate

(B), (C), (D) Arctic, Antarctic, Ecuador은 not mentioned

Q47 THING: Line Evidence

Answer Key : (D)

46번 문제의 key phrases인 "medieval volcanic eruptions", "equator", "Indonesia"가 등장하는 lines를 찾아보자. Lines 61–64에서 Gifford Miller는 Indonesia equator에서 volcano가 erupt했다고 주장한다.

Eliminate

(A), (B), (C) key phrases가 not mentioned

Q48 THING: Main Idea, Transition Word

Answer Key : (C)

Lines 68–71에서 "Another possible candidate ... is Ecuador's Quilotoa"라고 한다. "Another possible candidate"라고 한 것을 보면 과학자들이 Quilotoa 같은 다른 volcanic eruption들도 알고 있다는 것이다.

Eliminate

(A), (B), (D) volcanic eruptions 의 frequency나 effects, some volcanoes가 large calderas를 가지고 있다는 내용과 관련 없음

Q49 THING: Line Evidence

Answer Key : (D)

Lavigne's team이 Quilotoa의 eruption에대해 연구한 내용이 등장하는 lines를 찾아보자. Lines 71–75에서 "they didn't match the chemical composition of the glass"라며 "possible candidate" (line 68)이었던 Quilotoa가 왜 responsible for the Little Ice Age하지 않은지 보여준다.

Eliminate

(A), (B), (C) keyword인 Quilotoa가 not mentioned

Q50 THING: Graph

Answer Key : (C)

그래프를 잘 살펴보자. Average는 variation 값이 0일 때의 값이다. 따라서 그래프에서 greatest below-average temperature variation이 발생한 연도를 구하려면, 그래프의 수치가 0 이하로 가장 많이 떨어질 때의 연도를 보면 된다. 가장 가까운 연도는 1675년이다.

Eliminate

(A), (B), (D) not supported by graph

Q51 THING: Main Idea, Graph

Answer Key : (B)

Passage에서 lines 23–25를 보면 "between 1275 and 1300 CE"에 ice growth가 시작했다고 한다. 그리고 graph를 보면 1275 CE 즈음에 temperature가 떨어지기 시작했다는 것을 알 수 있다. 그러므로 보기 중에서 가장 가까운 연도는 1300 CE이다.

Eliminate

(A), (C), (D) not mentioned in passage/graph

Q52 THING: Graph

Answer Key : (A)

그래프를 잘 살펴보자. Medieval Warm Period의 temperature가 가장 높았던 연도는 1200 CE 즈음이다. 그리고 Little Ice Age의 "greatest cooling", 즉 온도가 가장 낮았던 연도는 1700 CE 즈음이다. 즉 temperature peaks 이후 몇 백 년이 흐른 후에 greatest cooling이 일어났다.

Eliminate

(B), (C), (D) not supported by graph

Section 2. Writing and Language Test

Q1
Answer : (B)
Category : Back Modifier
Explanation
"work"를 modify하는 back modifier이므로 relative pronoun인 "which"로 introduce해야 한다. 정답은 (B)
Eliminate
(A), (C), (D) back modifier를 introduce하는 relative pronoun이 없음

Q2
Answer : (B)
Category : Vocabulary
Explanation
"day"에 "mural"을 "paint"했다는 전 문장과 다르게 "night"에 "paint"했다는 다음 문장으로 transition하기 위해 contradiction을 나타내는 conjunctive adverb가 필요하다.
Eliminate
(A), (D) continuation을 나타내는 conjunction adverb
(C) "although"는 contradiction을 나타내는 adverb이지만 contradict하는 2개의 clause가 모두 뒤에 나와야 하므로 쓸 수 없음

Q3
Answer : (B)
Category : Various Comma Usages
Explanation
"the centerpiece"는 "final section of the mural"의 additional information이므로 전후에 comma를 쓴다.
Eliminate
(A), (C), (D) comma 사용하지 않음

Q4
Answer : (A)
Category : Insert/Delete/Replace
Explanation
이전 paragraph에서 "avoid scrutiny"한 이유를 설명하는 paragraph로 transition하는 문장이 필요하다. 정답은 (A)
Eliminate
(B), (C), (D) "avoid scrutiny"에 관해 이야기하지 않음

Q5
Answer : (D)
Category : Vocabulary
Explanation
숨겨져 있던 "mural"을 "공개한다"라는 뜻의 단어가 필요하다. 정답은 (D)
Eliminate
(A) "confided"의 뜻은 "털어놓다"
(B) "promulgated"의 뜻은 "널리 알리다"
(C) "inparted"의 뜻은 "전하다"

Q6
Answer : (B)
Category : Parallelism
Explanation
Subject가 같은 "was dominated"와 parallel한 included가 나와야 한다. 정답은 (B)
Eliminate
(A), (C), (D) "was discovered"와 parallel하지 않음

Q7

Answer : (D)

Category : Ambiguous Pronoun

Explanation

Antecedent가 unclear하기 때문에 정확한 단어를 써야 한다. 정답은 (D)

Eliminate

(A), (B) unclear antecedent

(C) ambiguous objective pronoun

Q8

Answer : (B)

Category : Wordiness

Explanation

"Chicago mural movement"에 focus하는 문장이 필요하다. 정답은 (B)

Eliminate

(A), (C), (D) wordy해서 "Chicago mural movement"에 focus하지 않음

Q9

Answer : (C)

Category : Parallelism, Wordiness

Explanation

"in abandoned lots", "on unused buildings" 와 같이 [preposition+adjective+noun]으로 parallel해야 한다. 정답은 (C)

Eliminate

(A), (B), (D) "in abandoned lots", "on unused buildings" 와 parallel하지 않아서 wordy

Q10

Answer : (A)

Category : Insert/Delete/Replace

Explanation

"America Tropical"이 전 문장의 "clean, restore, and repaint"하는 "restoration process"와 어떤 connection이 있는지 transition하는 문장이 필요하다. 정답은 (A)

Eliminate

(B), (C), (D) "America Tropical"과 "restoration process"의 connection을 보여주지 않음

Q11

Answer : (C)

Category : Insert/Delete/Replace

Explanation

2nd paragraph의 "Siqueiros's political message [...] work"와 같은 뜻의 문장이므로 필요 없다. 정답은 (C)

Eliminate

(A), (B) repetitive한 내용

(D) passage가 이미 support한 내용

Q12

Answer : (D)

Category : Logical Comparisons

Explanation

"originally grown crops"를 "conventionally grown counterparts"와 compare하는 것이기 때문에 아무 것도 필요하지 않다. 정답은 (D)

Eliminate

(A) "the people"과 compare하는 것이 아님

(B), (C) "the purchase of", "purchasing"과 compare하는 것이 아님

Q13

Answer : (B)
Category : Incomplete Sentences
Explanation
  문장의 main clause에 subject가 없는 sentence fragment이므로 subject가 필요하다. 정답은 (B)
Eliminate
  (A), (C), (D) subject가 없는 sentence fragment

Q14

Answer : (D)
Category : Wordiness
Explanation
  이미 passage에 나온 설명으로 imply할 수 있는 "conventional"한 방법의 설명은 필요 없다. 정답은 (D)
Eliminate
  (A) wordy
  (B) "conventional methods"가 "using pesticides and synthetic fertilizers"라는 것은 passage 전 내용으로 imply할 수 있음
  (C) "conventionally"가 "not organically"라는 것은 imply할 수 있음

Q15

Answer : (C)
Category : Vocabulary
Explanation
  "organic food"를 위해 "consumers"가 더 많은 돈을 spend한다는 전 내용을 contradict하도록 "organic food"가 "significant benefits"가 없다고 주장하는 다음 내용으로 transition하는 conjunctive adverb가 필요하다. 정답은 (C)
Eliminate
  (A), (B), (C) consequence와 continuation의 뜻의 conjunctive adverb

Q16

Answer : (C)
Category : Vocabulary
Explanation
  "advocates"가 "organic food"를 "계속 지지하다"라는 뜻의 단어가 필요하다. 정답은 (C)
Eliminate
  (A) "preserve"의 뜻은 "보존하다"
  (B) "carry on"의 뜻은 "계속 가다"
  (D) "sustain"의 뜻은 "지속시키다"

Q17

Answer : (A)
Category : Voabulary
Explanation
  "this assertion is not supported by scientific research"를 support하는 example을 provide하는 내용으로 transition하는 conjunctive adverb가 필요하다. 정답은 (A)
Eliminate
  (B) contradiction의 뜻의 conjunctive adverb
  (C) 다른 내용을 더 add하는 뜻의 conjunction phrase
  (D) 비슷한 내용을 introduce하는 conjunctive adverb

Q18

Answer : (C)
Category : Insert/Delete/Replace
Explanation
  "scientific evidence"의 example을 discuss하는 passage와 관련 없으므로 필요 없다. 정답은 (C)
Eliminate
  (A), (B) passage와 관련 없음
  (D) 흐름을 방해하는 문장이므로 "term"이 문제가 아님

Q19

Answer : (A)

Category : SVD - Basic

Explanation

문장의 subject인 "amounts"는 plural이므로 plural form verb를 써야 한다.

Eliminate

(B), (C), (D) singular form verb

Q20

Answer : (C)

Category : Insert/Delete/Replace

Explanation

"nonorganic food"를 support하는 문장이 필요하다. 정답은 (C)

Eliminate

(A), (B), (D) "nonorganic food와 관련 없음

Q21

Answer : (B)

Category : SVD - Basic, Diction

Explanation

"있다"라는 뜻의 [there+be]가 필요하며 subject가 "numerous other reasons"이기 때문에 plural form verb가 필요하다. 정답은 (B)

Eliminate

(A) diction error

(C), (D) plural verb

Q22

Answer : (D)

Category : Period, Semi-colon vs. Comma, Various Comma Usages

Explanation

"such as"는 앞에 나온 "reasons"의 example을 introduce하기 때문에 중간에 punctuation이 있을 수 없다. 정답은 (D)

Eliminate

(A), (B), (C) "such as" 뒤에 punctuation 사용할 수 없음

Q23

Answer : (C)

Category : Vocabulary

Explanation

"interest"를 표현하는 postive한 뜻의 "흥미롭다"라는 단어가 필요하다. 정답은 (C)

Eliminate

(A) "life–altering"의 뜻은 "인생을 바꾸는"

(B) "galvanizing"의 뜻은 "충격적인"

(D) "weird"의 뜻은 "기이한"

Q24

Answer : (C)

Category : Idioms

Explanation

[not only...but also...]의 idiomatic expression이므로 but also를 써야 한다. 정답은 (C)

Eliminate

(A), (B), (D) correct idiomatic expression이 아님

Q25

Answer : (B)

Category : Insert/Delete/Replace

Explanation

다음 paragraph가 "human–intensive data collection"의 example과 importance를 discuss하므로 supportive하고 positive한 문장이 필요하다. 정답은 (B)

Eliminate

(A) 다음 passage 내용과 다름

(C) 같은 문장의 "new avenues"가 다른 options

(D) "human–intensive data collection"을 support하지 않음

Q26

Answer : (D)

Category : Redundancy

Explanation

"scholars"를 두 번 말하는 것은 redundant하기 때문에 subjective relative pronoun을 사용하여 바로 문장을 이을 수 있다. 정답은 (D)

Eliminate

 (A), (B), (C) redundant

Q27

Answer : (C)

Category : Content Order

Explanation

"Data gathering"에 관한 내용이므로 "data"에 관한 자세한 내용의 sentence 4 뒤에 넣어서 sentence 5로의 transition을 complete해야 한다. 정답은 (C)

Eliminate

 (A), (B), (D) paragraph의 흐름을 방해함

Q28

Answer : (A)

Category : SVD

Explanation

문장의 subject 인 "research"는 uncountable noun이기 때문에 singular form verb를 써야 한다. 정답은 (A)

Eliminate

 (B), (C), (D) plural form verb

Q29

Answer : (D)

Category : Colons and Dahses

Explanation

"the vast array [...] media"는 "army"에 관한 information을 담은 내용이고 incomplete sentence이기 때문에 colon를 써서 introduce해야 한다. 정답은 (D)

Eliminate

(A) 다른 내용이기 때문에 중간에 punctuation이 필요함

(B) "be replaced by"는 idiomatic expression 이기 때문에 중간에 dash를 쓸 수 없음

(C) transiton하는 것이 아니므로 semi–colon은 쓸 수 없음

Q30

Answer : (B)

Category : Diction

Explanation

소셜 미디어 사이트의 "site"가 맞는 단어이고 [in search of ...]는 idiomatic expression이다. 정답은 (B)

Eliminate

(A), (C), (D) "cite"와 "in search for"는 correct meaning이 아님

Q31

Answer : (C)

Category : Graph (Map)

Explanation

Map에서 middle과 western 쪽에 pop, south에 coke, 그리고 northeast와 southwest에 soda가 쓰이는 것으로 표시되어 있다. 정답은 (C)

Eliminate

(A), (B), (D) map의 내용과 맞지 않음

Q32

Answer : (B)

Category : Diction

Explanation

"their"가 3rd person plural possessive pronoun의 correct diction이다. 정답은 (B)

Eliminate

(A), (C), (D) correct diction이 아님

Q33
Answer : (A)
Category : Insert/Delete/Replace
Explanation
   Data collection에 관한 passage이므로 "data"에 관련된 문장이 필요하다. 정답은 (A)
Eliminate
   (B), (C), (D) passage와 관련 없음

Q34
Answer : (C)
Category : Tense Context
Explanation
   [a numer of+noun]은 singular form verb를 사용하고 문장의 다른 verb들이 present tense이기 때문에 present tense인 singular form verb를 써야 한다. 정답은 (C)
Eliminate
   (A), (B), (D) present tense와 singular form이 아님

Q35
Answer : (C)
Category : Colons and Dashes
Explanation
   문장을 중간에 interrupt하고 "fundamental elements"를 list한 것이기 때문에 앞뒤에 dash를 넣어야 한다. 정답은 (C)
Eliminate
   (A) 중간에 colon을 넣으면 "and is thus [...] game"을 colon 전 clause와 connect할 수 없음
   (B) 앞에 colon을 넣고 dash로 끝낼 수 없음
   (D) 문장 중간의 additional information 앞뒤에 semi-colon을 넣을 수 없음

Q36
Answer : (B)
Category : Conjunctions vs. Conjunctive Adverbs
Explanation
   "however"는 conjunction이 아닌 conjunctive adverb이기 때문에 2 clauses를 connect할 수 없다. 정답은 (B)
Eliminate
   (A), (B), (D) "however"는 2 clauses를 connect 할 수 없음

Q37
Answer : (D)
Category : Insert/Delete/Replace
Explanation
   "successful communication"에 관한 내용은 앞 문장과 같은 내용이기 때문에 필요 없다. 정답은 (D)
Eliminate
   (A), (B), (C) 앞 문장의 내용과 같아서 필요 없음

Q38
Answer : (A)
Category : Insert/Delete/Replace
Explanation
   "communicating"에 관련된 passage이므로 그와 관련된 내용의 문장이 필요하다. 정답은 (A)
Eliminate
   (B), (C), (D) passage와 관련 없음

Q39
Answer : (C)
Category : Vocabulary
Explanation
   왜 "game designer must be skilled writers and speakers"인지 앞 문장이 explain하고 있으므로 result를 뜻하는 conjunctive adverb가 필요하다. 정답은 (C)

Eliminate

(A) similarity를 뜻하는 conjunctive adverb

(B), (D) contradiction을 뜻하는 conjunctive adverb

Q40

Answer : (B)

Category : Number Agreement

Explanation

"a video game"은 singular noun이므로 "writer and speaker"도 singular이어야 한다. 정답은 (B)

Eliminate

(A), (C), (D) plural nouns

Q41

Answer : (D)

Category : Vocabulary, Redundancy

Explanation

"programmers"는 job이기 때문에 가장 정확한 "career"라는 표현을 사용해야 한다. 정답은 (D)

Eliminate

(A), (C) "programmers"가 무엇인지 clear하지 않음

(B) "start"와 "begin"은 synonymous함

Q42

Answer : (D)

Category : Vocabulary

Explanation

"courses in psychology and human behavior"가 "중요한" "collarboration skills"를 "develop"한다는 뜻의 단어가 필요하다. 정답은 (D)

Eliminate

(A) "emphatic"의 뜻은 "강조하는"

(B) "paramount"의 뜻은 "최고의"

(C) "eminent"의 뜻은 "저명한"

Q43

Answer : (A)

Category : Front Modifier

Explanation

"demanding and deadline driven"은 "video game design"을 choose하는 것이 아닌 "video game design"을 modify한다. 정답은 (A)

Eliminate

(B), (C), (D) "demanding and deadline driven"이 modify하지 않음

Q44

Answer : (B)

Category : Content Order

Explanation

"designer"가 필요한 또 다른 quality에 대한 내용이므로 "computer programming"이 필요하다는 내용의 sentence 1 뒤에 와야 한다. 정답은 (B)

Eliminate

(A), (C), (D) passage의 흐름을 방해함

Section 3. Math Test
(No Calculator)

Q1
Answer : (A)
Category : Absolute Value
Explanation
 Absolute value는 괄호 안에 무엇이 있든지 간에 positive number로 change하기 때문에, expression이 0으로 되려면 equal sign 반대쪽엔 positive sign을 가진 숫자가 있어야 한다.
 ∴ A

Q2
Answer : (A)
Category : Functions
Explanation
$f(6) = \frac{3}{2}x + b = 7, \ b = -2$
$f(-2) = \frac{3}{2}x - 2 = -5$
 ∴ A

Q3
Answer : (A)
Category : Equations
Explanation
$x = 6y \ \rightarrow \ 4(y+1) = 6y$
 ∴ A

Q4
Answer : (B)
Category : Functions
Explanation
$f(x) = -2x + 5 \ \rightarrow \ f(-3x) = -2(-3x) + 5$
 ∴ B

Q5
Answer : (C)
Category : Equations
Explanation
$3(2x+1)(4x+1) \ \rightarrow \ (6x+3)(4x+1)$
$\rightarrow 24x^2 + 12x + 6x + 3$
 ∴ C

Q6
Answer : (B)
Category : Fractions
Explanation
$\frac{(a-b)}{b} = \frac{a}{b} - 1 = \frac{3}{7}$
 ∴ B

Q7
Answer : (D)
Category : Fractions
Explanation
 16번째 주에 26 miles를 뛰고, 4번째 주에 8 mile을 뛰면, 12주 안에 18 mile을 더 뛰는 것이기 때문에, 매주 1.5 mile씩 늘렸다는 것을 알 수 있다.
 ∴ D

Q8
Answer : (A)
Category : Equations
Explanation
 Line이 parallel하므로 slope가 같아야 한다.
 ∴ A

Q9

Answer : (D)

Category : Powers and Roots

Explanation

$\sqrt{x-a}=x-4 \rightarrow \sqrt{x-2}=x-4$
$\rightarrow x-2=(x-4)^2 \rightarrow x-2=x^2-8x+16$
$\rightarrow 0=x^2-9x+18 \rightarrow 0=(x-3)(x-6)$

하지만 $x=3$을 기존 equation에 apply하면,
$\sqrt{1}=\sqrt{-1}$라는 틀린 solution이 나온다.

$\therefore$ D

Q10

Answer : (D)

Category : Fractions

Explanation

$\dfrac{t+5}{t-5}=10 \rightarrow t+5=10t-50$

$\therefore$ D

Q11

Answer : (C)

Category : Equations

Explanation

$x=2((2x-3)(x+9))+5 \rightarrow 4x^2+30x-54$

$4x^2+30x-54=0$이고, 이 equation의 discriminant가 positive이므로, 이 equation은 2 distinct roots가 있다.

$\therefore$ C

Q12

Answer : (C)

Category : Percentage, Equations

Explanation

Price of Ken's sandwich가 x라고 가정하면, price of Paul's sandwich는 $(x+1)$이다. 두 개의 sandwich들의 합은 $x+(x+1)=2x+1$이고, 두 part로 나누면 한 명당 $x+0.5$인 것을 알 수 있다. 그 값에 tip의 값을 더하면

$x+0.5+0.2(x+0.5)=1.2(x+0.5)=1.2x+0.6$

$\therefore$ C

Q13

Answer : (B)

Category : Functions

Explanation

$f(x)=g(x)$일 때 intersect한다.

$8x^2-2=-8x^2+2 \rightarrow x=\pm\dfrac{1}{2}$

k와 k가 있지만, 문제는 k의 값을 구하는 것이므로,

$\therefore$ B

Q14

Answer : (A)

Category : Numbers, Fractions

Explanation

$\dfrac{8-i}{3-2i}$를 standard form인 $a+bi$로 쓰려면, $3-2i$의 conjugate와 곱해야 한다.

$\left(\dfrac{8-i}{3-2i}\right)\left(\dfrac{3+2i}{3+2i}\right)=\dfrac{24+16i-3i+(-i)(2i)}{3^2-(2i)^2}$

$i^2=-1$이므로,

$\dfrac{24+16i-3i+2}{3^2-(-4)^2}=\dfrac{26+13i}{13}$

$\therefore$ A

Q15

Answer : (B)

Category : Equations

Explanation

$x^2-\dfrac{k}{2}x=2p \rightarrow 0=2x^2-kx-4p$

Quadratic formula를 적용하면

$\dfrac{-b\pm\sqrt{b^2-4ac}}{2a}$, $a=2$, $b=-k$, $c=-4p$

$\therefore$ B

Q16

Answer : 9

Category : Equations

Explanation

Ratio에 따라서 height를 각각 $2h$, $3h$, h라고 하면
$2h+3h+h=18$
→ $h=3$
∴ $3\times 3=9$

Q17

Answer : 6 or $\dfrac{3}{5}$

Category : Triangles

Explanation

x와 y는 right triangle의 acute angles이다. 그러므로, 둘은 complementary angle이고, sine 과 cosine의 complementary angle relationship은 $\sin x = \cos y$이므로,
∴ 6 or $\dfrac{3}{5}$

Q18

Answer : 5

Category : Equations

Explanation

$x^3 - 5x^2 + 2x - 10 = 0$
→ $(x^3 - 5x^2) + (2x - 10) = 0$
→ $x^2(x-5) + 2(x-5) = 0$
→ $(x-5)(x^2+2) = 0$
$x=5$ or $x = \pm i\sqrt{2}$
real value of x이므로
∴ 5

Q19

Answer : 0

Category : Equations

Explanation

$-3x + 4y = 20$ ······ ①
$6x + 3y = 15$ ······ ②
② $+ 2\times$ ① → $y=5$, $x=0$
∴ 0

Q20

Answer : 25

Category : Fractions

Explanation

30 kilometer의 차이에서, 75℃ 의 difference가 생긴다는 것을 알 수 있다. $-\dfrac{75}{30} = -\dfrac{2.5}{1}$ 이므로, 1 kilometer마다 2.5℃ 가 떨어진다는 것을 알 수 있다. 하지만 k는 10 kilometers마다의 decrease를 나타내기 때문에,

$\dfrac{2.5℃}{1\ kilometer} \times 10\ kilometers$

∴ 25

Section 4. Math Test
(Calculator)

Q1
Answer : (B)
Category : Equations
Explanation
x가 number of movies라고 가정하면,
$1.50x + 9.80 = 12.80$
$x = 2$
∴ B

Q2
Answer : (C)
Category : Equations
Explanation
m이 number of months라고 가정하면, "increase his typing speed by 5 words per minute each month"는 $5m$이다. 현재 Donald가 180 word per minute을 칠 수 있으므로, $180 + 5m$이 "the number of words per minute that Donald will be able to type m months from now"를 표현한다.
∴ C

Q3
Answer : (C)
Category : Fractions
Explanation
$3 \text{ pounds} \times \frac{1}{2} \times \frac{1}{3} \times \frac{16 \text{ ounces}}{1 \text{ pound}} = 8 \text{ ounces}$
∴ C

Q4
Answer : (B)
Category : Percentage
Explanation
$225 \times 0.256 = 57.6$
∴ B

Q5
Answer : (B)
Category : Equations
Explanation
$D = \frac{m}{v} \rightarrow m = 24g, D = \frac{3g}{1 \text{ milliliter}}$
$\frac{3g}{1 \text{ milliliter}} = \frac{24g}{v}$
∴ B

Q6
Answer : (A)
Category : Equations
Explanation
Angelica가 일한 시간을 a로 가정하면, Raul이 일한 시간은 $a + 11$이다. 그러므로 둘의 합은 $a + (a + 11)$이고, $2a + 11 = 59$이므로,
∴ A

Q7
Answer : (A)
Category : Fractions
Explanation
$\frac{\text{Number of comedies with a PG-13 rating}}{\text{Total number of all movies}} = \frac{4}{50}$
∴ A

Q8

Answer : (D)
Category : Equations
Explanation

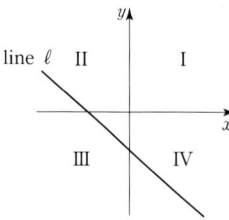

Line l이 Quadrants II, III, IV를 모두 포함하려면 slope가 negative이어야 한다.
∴ D

Q9

Answer : (B)
Category : Fractions
Explanation

Probability
$$= \frac{(\text{Midwest } 18 \text{ to } 24) + (\text{Midwest } 25 \text{ to } 44)}{(18 \text{ to } 24) + (25 \text{ to } 44)}$$
$$\frac{14690}{62662} \approx 0.234$$
∴ B

Q10

Answer : (A)
Category : Problem Solving and Data Analysi
Explanation

그래프를 보고 longest gestation period를 표기하는 point를 찾으면 그 point의 $y-$axis인 life expectancy를 찾을 수 있다.
∴ A

Q11

Answer : (A)
Category : Fractions
Explanation

Ratio of life expectancy to gestation period는
$\frac{\text{Life expectancy}}{\text{Gestation period}}$ 로 표기할 수 있다. Fraction은 numerator가 클수록, denominator가 작을수록 값이 커진다.
∴ A

Q12

Answer : (C)
Category : Functions
Explanation

Function의 $x-$intercept는 function이 0과 같을 때의 x 값이다.
∴ C

Q13

Answer : (C)
Category : Problem Solving and Data Analysis
Explanation

Population of mosquitoes가 매 5주마다 a factor of 10으로 increase한다. 이 relationship은
$P(t) = 100(10)^{\frac{t}{5}}$
∴ C

Q14

Answer : (D)
Category : Equations
Explanation

Money generated at an interest rate of 5%
$= 1000\left(1 + \frac{5}{1,200}\right)^{12}$

money generated at an interest rate of 3%
$= 1000\left(1 + \frac{3}{1,200}\right)^{12}$ 답은 이 둘의 difference이다.
∴ D

Q15
Answer : (B)
Category : Functions
Explanation

Exponential equation인 $y=ax^b$에서 a는 $y-$intercept를, b는 increase 또는 decrease를 나타낸다. 그러므로 positive a, negative b는 positive $y-$axis와 exponential decay를 뜻한다.

∴ B

Q16
Answer : (A)
Category : Equations
Explanation

x가 number of days라고 가정하면, Store A에서 빌리는 값은 $y=750+(15+65)x$, Store B에서 빌리는 값은 $y=600+(25+80)x$.
Store B의 총 가격이 Store A의 총 가격보다 낮거나 같으려면 $600+105x \leq 750+80x$

∴ A

Q17
Answer : (D)
Category : Equations
Explanation

Total cost $y=M+(W+K)x$를 그래프로 그리면 $W+K$가 slope이므로,

∴ D

Q18
Answer : (C)
Category : Solids
Explanation

하나의 drinking glass의 volume은
$\pi r^2 h = \pi \left(\dfrac{3}{2}\right)^2 6 \approx 42.41$ cubic inches로 구해진다.

"Total number of glasses Jim can pour from 1 gallon"

$= \dfrac{\text{number of cubic inches in 1 gallon}}{\text{number of cubic inches in 1 glass}}$

$= \dfrac{231}{42.41}$

하지만 문제는 "full glasses"를 묻고 있으므로,

∴ C

Q19
Answer : (A)
Category : Equations
Explanation

$3p-2 \geq 1$ ······ ①
①$+4 \rightarrow 3p+2 \geq 5$

∴ A

Q20
Answer : (C)
Category : Functions
Explanation

Biomass가 매해마다 두 배로 늘어난다면, graph는 increasing exponential slope를 보여야 한다.

∴ C

Q21
Answer : (C)
Category : Problem Solving and Data Analysis
Explanation

Scatterplot의 정확한 point들은 예측할 수 없지만, point가 line $y=x$보다 높으려면, y의 value가 x의 value보다 높아야 한다.

∴ C

Q22

Answer : (B)

Category : Percentage, Problem Solving and Data Analysis

Explanation

Percent decrease →

$\dfrac{\text{Original value} - \text{New value}}{\text{Original value}} \times 100\%$ →

$\dfrac{2.25 - 2.00}{2.25} \times 100\% \approx 11.1\%$

∴ B

Q23

Answer : (B)

Category : Problem Solving and Data Analysis

Explanation

Standard deviation은 data가 평균에서 얼마나 떨어져 있는지의 measure이다. City A의 평균은 78.8이고, City B의 평균은 78.0이다. City A의 data는 대부분 평균에 근접하지만, City B의 data는 평균값에서 멀다.

∴ B

Q24

Answer : (C)

Category : Circles

Explanation

Segment AB가 diameter이므로, arc $\widehat{ADB}$는 semicircle인 것을 알 수 있다.

Circle의 circumference는 그러므로 $\widehat{ADB}$의 두 배인 16π이고, circumference $= 2\pi r$이므로,

$r = \dfrac{16\pi}{2\pi} = 8$

∴ C

Q25

Answer : (B)

Category : Functions

Explanation

$f(x) = 2x^3 + 6x^2 + 4x$

→ $f(x) = 2x(x^2 + 3x + 2)$

→ $f(x) = 2x \times g(x)$

$p(x) = 2x \times g(x) + 3g(x)$

$p(x) = g(x)(2x + 3)$

∴ B

Q26

Answer : (C)

Category : Equations

Explanation

$-y < x < y$이므로 x의 값은 y와 0 사이이거나 0과 y 사이이므로, $|x| < y$

그리고 $-y < x < y$가 $-y < y$를 뜻하므로

∴ C

Q27

Answer : (D)

Category : Problem Solving and Data Analysis

Explanation

Equation $y = 0.0125x + 61$에서

x는 x-axis인 population density이고,

그 x가 0일 때 y-intercept가 61인 것으로 보아,

61은 population density가 0일 때,

relative housing cost가 61%를 나타내는 것을 알 수 있다. 그 뜻은 population density가 굉장히 낮을 때에도 적어도 61%의 cost라는 것이다.

∴ D

Q28

Answer : (D)

Category : Functions

Explanation

Function이 minimum value를 갖게 하려면 vertex form이어야 한다.

$f(x) = x^2 + 2x - 24 =$
$(x^2 + 2x + 1) - 1 - 24 = (x+1)^2 - 25$

∴ D

Q29

Answer : (B)

Category : Problem Solving and Data Analysis

Explanation

$x = \dfrac{m+9}{2}$, $y = \dfrac{2m+15}{2}$, $z = \dfrac{3m+18}{2}$

x, y, z의 average는 $\dfrac{x+y+z}{3} \rightarrow$

$\dfrac{\dfrac{m+9}{2} + \dfrac{2m+15}{2} + \dfrac{3m+18}{2}}{3} \rightarrow \dfrac{6m+42}{6}$

∴ B

Q30

Answer : (D)

Category : Functions

Explanation

$f(x) = k$가 세 개의 real solution을 가지려면 $y = k$가 $f(x)$와 세 개의 intersection을 가져야 한다. 보기 중에서 그 조건에 해당하는 답은 $y = -3$ 뿐이다.

∴ D

Q31

Answer : 1160

Category : Rate

Explanation

"Water in the pool after 70 minutes"

$= \left(\dfrac{8 \text{ gallons}}{1 \text{ minute}} \times 70 \text{ minutes} \right) + 600$

∴ 1160

Q32

Answer : $\dfrac{1}{2}$ or .5

Category : Equations

Explanation

x year old male: $P = \dfrac{x+220}{2}$

$\rightarrow P = \dfrac{1}{2}x + 110$

$(x+1)$ year old male:

$P = \dfrac{(x+1)+220}{2} \rightarrow P = \left(\dfrac{1}{2}x + 110\right) + \dfrac{1}{2}$

∴ $\dfrac{1}{2}$ or .5

Q33

Answer : 4.55

Category : Fractions

Explanation

1 pes = 11.65 inches = 16 digits

75 digits = $\dfrac{11.65 \text{ \sout{inches}}}{16 \text{ \sout{digits}}} = \dfrac{1 \text{ foot}}{12 \text{ \sout{inches}}}$

∴ 4.55

Q34

Answer : 150

Category : Fractions, Percentage

Explanation

"$\dfrac{3}{5}$ of the total number of bats in the study are male"이 true statement 이려면,

$\dfrac{\text{male bats}}{\text{total bats}} = \dfrac{240+x}{500+x} = \dfrac{3}{5}$ 이어야 한다.

∴ 150

Q35

Answer : 2.25 or $\dfrac{9}{4}$

Category : Fractions, Ratio

Explanation

q_s가 dynamic pressure of the slower fluid moving with velocity v_s로 가정하고, q_f가 dynamic pressure of the faster fluid moving with velocity v_f로 가정한다면, $v_f = 1.5v_s$이다.

$q_f = \dfrac{1}{2}nv_f^2 \rightarrow q_f = \dfrac{1}{2}n(1.5v_s)^2 \rightarrow$

$q_f = (2.25)\dfrac{1}{2}nv_s^2 \rightarrow q_f = (2.25)q_s$

$\dfrac{q_f}{q_s} = \dfrac{2.25q_s}{q_s}$

$\therefore 2.25$ or $\dfrac{9}{4}$

Q36

Answer : 29, 30, 31, 32, 33 or 34

Category : Circles

Explanation

Radius가 10이므로, circumference는 20π이다.

$\dfrac{x}{360} = \dfrac{2}{20\pi}$, or $x = \dfrac{360}{20\pi}s$, $5 < s < 6$이므로

$\dfrac{360}{20\pi}(5) < x < \dfrac{360}{20\pi}(6) \rightarrow 28.6 < x < 34.4$

$\therefore$ 29, 30, 31, 32, 33 or 34

Q37

Answer : 0.72

Category : Functions

Explanation

r은 stock의 한 주 후의 value를 나타내므로, 매주 28%가 떨어지는 stock의 한 주 후의 value는

$V - (0.28)V = (0.72)V$

$\therefore 0.72$

Q38

Answer : 134

Category : Functions

Explanation

$V = 360(0.72)^t = 360(.72)^3$

$\therefore 134$